Look What These People Have to Say About *Turbulence!*

"I love this book! Smooth, easy to read, really informative. The writing has an edge that held my attention from cover to cover!"

Sandy Vilas
Author of *Power Networking*

"Turbulence is a good word to describe rough flying conditions and the current business environment for most companies today. Roger Herman puts a new perspective on what you might do in your company to smooth out the years ahead.

Gordon M. Bethune
President & Chief Executive Officer
Continental Airlines, Inc.

"Our human future is inextricably interwoven with our technological future. A dedicated competent workforce is essential to develop new technologies and bring them to market. Employers and employees would be wise to read and absorb what Roger Herman explores in *Turbulence!*

Dr. Daniel Burrus, Technology Forecaster
and Author of *Technotrends*

"Straightforward, no nonsense. Herman's report of what's coming is insightful, informative, and thought-provoking. I recommend *Turbulence!* as a valuable guide for business leaders who want to stay on the leading edge of work issues."

Robert Mayer Evans, President
Global Trends Institute and
former Moscow Bureau Chief, **CBS News**

"The economic boom--in the United States and internationally-- will stimulate major changes in the world of work. We'll definitely do business differently than we have in the past. Anyone investing in his/her personal or corporate future should learn about the trends and forecasts covered in *Turbulence!* I'll advise my clients to read Herman's latest."

Harry S. Dent, Jr., author,
The Great Boom Ahead

"$2-\frac{3}{4}$ cheers for *Turbulence!* I don't agree with everything Roger says, but then futurists rarely agree on everything. His thoughts are provocative, insightful, and educational. This book is a fine contribution to futurist literature."

Marvin J. Cetron, President
Forecasting International and
author of *American Renaissance*

"Roger Herman shares some powerful insights in *Turbulence!* I heartily recommend it to anyone serious about negotiating his/her future career positioning. Valuable for anyone running a business today."

Somers White, CMC, CSP, CPAE

"Roger Herman is again right on target. *Turbulence!* is must reading for those close to retirement as well as for those just entering the workforce. Every executive, manager, and human resource professional should read this book!"

Catherine D. Fyock, CSP, SPHR
author of *Unretirement, Get the Best,* and
America's Workforce is Coming of Age

"Outstanding...Full of wise, useable ideas. A clear, concise and pragmatic answer to the question 'What's happening?'"

Gene Greissman, author of
The New Achievers

"Roger outlines important changes that affect everyone who works or runs an organization. *Turbulence!* is packed with valuable, inspiring information. Anyone who reads it has the powerful tools needed to shape job, career and company wisely for the next decade. Read it and open your mind to the exciting possibilities that lie ahead!"

Paula Ancona, national columnist and
author of *SuccessAbilities!*

Managers who wish to be employed at the end of this decade need to read *Turbulence!* Learn how to become an "Adaptable" or risk being overrun by these compelling trends.

John J. Anderson III
Director, Technology Assessment &
Planning, **Weyerhauser Corporation**

Turbulence! should be required reading for every executive in America! Roger Herman's visionary perspectives will empower corporate leaders to make more informed decisions about present and future strategies.

Bernard Appel
Former President
Radio Shack/Tandy Corporation

In an overwhelming world of data, Roger Herman has identified and distilled the trends that will influence business practices and direction during the next decade. I enjoyed the emphasis on individuals' need to manage their careers and not depend on the employer for direction. *Turbulence!* is certainly an eye-opener for those who believe that their future success will be driven by the same competencies as their current success.

Chad Cook, Manager of
Organizational Development
Rubbermaid, Incorporated

Roger E. Herman is right on target with what he predicts, just as he was in *Keeping Good People*. Read *Turbulence!* It will help prepare you to cope with the unpredictable now and down the road. And it will show you how you can manage successfully in what's sure to be a continuously turbulent workplace.

Jack Gillespie, Executive Producer,
Newstrack Executive Tape Service

Here in Southern California, we've already begun to experience some of what Roger Herman talks about in his new book. *Turbulence!* is a good word to describe what's happening. His advice helped position our company for a more profitable, exciting future. I recommend *Turbulence!* to every retailer—except our competitors.

Daniel W. Vengler, President
Daniel's Markets, San Diego

The turbulent times are just starting. Prepare! Prepare! For the future belongs to those who prepare for it. **First Step**: Read *Turbulence!* now.

Martin Edelston, President
Boardroom, Inc.

Turbulence!

Challenges and Opportunities in the World of Work

Are You Prepared For the Future?

Turbulence!

Challenges and Opportunities in the World of Work

Are You Prepared for the Future?

Roger E. Herman

Oakhill Press
Akron, Ohio ⋏ New York

Turbulence!

Library of Congress Cataloging-in-Publication Data

Herman, Roger E., 1943-
    Turbulence! : Challenges and Opportunities in the
World of Work: Are you prepared? / Roger E. Herman.

  Includes index
  ISBN 1-886939-01-2 (hc) : $22.95
  1. Work - Forecasting. 2. Manpower planning--United
States--Forecasting.   I. Title.
HD4901.H43   1995
331--dc20   95-13198
                                          CIP

0 9 8 7 6 5 4 3 2 1

FIRST EDITION

First Printing, September 1995

Turbulence!

Contents

Section 1
The Trends

Section 2
Influencing Factors

Section 3
Forecasts

v

Section 4
Implications and Opportunities

Dedication

Each of us is influenced by many people in our lives. Some people impress us because they are so strong, so knowledgeable, and so dedicated to who they are and what they do.

In my early writing days, I met a young man who taught me and encouraged me. Greg Bethel was immersed in his love--books. His delightful bookstore, Pickwick Books, Inc. was unique, inviting, and eclectic. So was Greg.

My conversations with Greg inspired me to become a serious writer of books, not just magazine and journal articles. I gained a greater appreciation of the book business and how much people appreciate a well-written book.

Greg lived life to the fullest, right up to the time cancer snatched him from us in 1993. His 38 years were invested well. Greg Bethel is remembered by many people whose lives were touched by this extraordinary young man.

Acknowledgments

"No man is an island."
                    John Donne

This old adage certainly applies to writing a book. It is the author's responsibility to craft the work so others may benefit from the creative work. But the actual brain work and writing is only part of the picture.

A book like *Turbulence!* requires a lot of research and collaborative thinking with colleagues. It requires lots of research and thinking time, with cognitive interaction to integrate and refine ideas. It is a challenge for any busy person to find unfettered time to work with minimal interruption so that ideas flow smoothly from thought to paper.

Along the way, the critical reviews of knowledgeable, objective people has helped assure contact with reality. Authors can easily get so wrapped up in their work process that it's practically impossible to see blatant errors of omission or commission.

It is altogether fitting and proper to acknowledge those who helped make *Turbulence!* possible.

First, a blanket salute and appreciation to my fellow members of the World Future Society. Our conversations at conferences, during personal visits, and over the phone have always been stimulating. A special thanks to other Professional Members of the

Society. Your deep thinking and challenges keep me on my toes.

A special thank-you goes to Joe Coates of Coates & Jarratt, Washington, D. C. and Marvin Cetron of Forecasting International, Arlington, Virginia. These two leaders in the futures field have been especially helpful.

Dorothy Jackson of the US Bureau of the Census and her former colleague, George Dailey, provided insights and information that helped spawn this book. A number of other researchers and experts in various government departments stimulated and expanded my thinking with their perspectives.

Thanks go to my clients for their support and openness in my exploration of trends in the real world. Each of my clients provides a laboratory for me to insure my theories are solidly anchored in reality.

Estelle Herman provided her sharpened-pencil editing services so this book would be more readable. Miss Hardy and Miss Vincent did a fine job teaching me how to put words together, but I never stop learning how to do it better.

Finally, my sincere appreciation to fellow futurist and working partner, Joyce L. Gioia, CMC, whose insight, critical thinking, and intellectual challenges have helped make this book a success. And many thanks to our publisher, Marty James, at Oakhill for his patience and good humor, which made this project an enjoyable experience.

Foreword

In a world awash with information, skill in communication is much to be cherished. Some have that gift, some can only strive for it, and others must remain envious. Roger E. Herman's gift is the ability to take complex material generated in an academic think tank, a government milieu, or the real world of corporate business, and make it lively, personal, and totally understandable.

Turbulence! demonstrates Herman's skills at work. His terminology, while not always standard for futures research, does stick in your mind. "Corporate Cocooning" is likely to become a new catch phrase for those who understand and use the concept. "Reverse apprenticeships" and "high productivity/high stress" each grasp a truth in a way that makes it ways to talk about and hence facilitate communication.

I'm not sure that I agree with Herman's section on "The New Breed: The Adaptables," but surely the concept draws together strands of development in a way that captures important implications. It would be hard to avoid reviewing trends in the areas that he does without addressing the question of the adaptables as a new breed.

Win, lose, or draw, Herman has put in front of us tasty, well-prepared food for thought. It is unusual for an author writing on human resources to run the spectrum from corporate implications to advice to young people, while sandwiching in between these common sense advice on positioning yourself, as an individual, for the future.

My hope is that readers share my engagement with Roger Herman's interpretation of current thoughts on our emerging turbulent workplace.

Joseph F. Coates
Coates & Jarratt, Inc., Futurists
Washington, D. C.

Co-author of *FutureWork,*
Issues Management,
and *What Futurists Believe*

Introduction

In the past 25 years, the United States has encountered some if its most difficult challenges. Because the United States enjoyed an unparalleled strength in the world market, we could, for a time, afford to delay our responses to these challenges. But, as we have learned, unresolved problems grow ever larger. As the end of the twentieth century draws nearer, our grace period is running out. We must either begin solving the problems we've neglected or commit ourselves to a decline almost impossible to reverse. *Turbulence!* will help us prepare, let us know what kind of changes are ahead as well as offering advice on how to meet those changes with foresight and understanding.

One major shift, and it's spelled out beautifully, is the shift away from traditional worksites and styles. With the growing popularity of flextime and flexspace, with the advent of the electronic/virtual office, the whole dynamic of work and management is going to be tested and stressed. And what of those good employees who are currently at work? Will they want to stay?

What do companies need to do to attract and keep good people? What will our roles be in five years time? Where will our jobs be in the next decade? *Turbulence!* provides insights for executives, managers, entrepreneurs, anyone working or looking for work in this chaotic, trend-influenced market.

Turbulence! is a good defense against the uncertainty of the changing world of work. In it, Roger Herman has taken a close look not only at the problems and trends facing our society, but at the solutions being pioneered by innovative educators, futurists, and businesspeople. He's studied what works, and why mistakes can cause an otherwise promising business to fail. The end result is part reporting, part analysis, part prescription and very readable.

Marvin J. Cetron, President
Forecasting International and
author of *American Renaissance,*
Educational Renaissance,
and other books on the future

1

Overview

"Those who do not prepare for the future are destined to be its victims."

Scholars and sages have echoed this warning, in one form or another, for centuries. Those who listened, survived . . . many even prospered. Those who refused to heed the warning became victims. Victims of their own shortsightedness. Often they were victims of their own personal agendas.

For years leaders, and their advisors, have bandied about words like "vision" and "strategic planning." In too many organizations, these terms get only "lip service." Planning and thinking into the future are rarely taken seriously. Too often when visionary planning is done, the results have no connection with the current reality of the host organization.

Those forward thinkers who do speak up are usually ignored, as leaders go where they want to go anyway. When egos or politics enter the equation, the investment in future planning is ignored. The consequences are what you might expect: the crippling or eventual demise of the entire organization.

Unfortunately, most organizations are led—er, managed—on a relatively short-term platform. For-profit corporations concentrate on the bottom line—profits, net worth, stockholder dividends—at the end of the period. That period may be a day, month, quarter, or year. Thinking is rarely extended beyond a year in managing the business flow.

Government agencies usually respond to the pressures of the moment. They are more reactive than forward-thinking. Their foresight extends to the next election when directions may change again.

Not-for-profits are forced to focus on the time period for which they have—or must—collect moneys to keep the doors open. Some have gotten into some longer-range program planning, but they're hampered by the uncertainty of funding.

When they do think further into the future, their planning is generally accomplished in a vacuum.

Long-term businesses can't be run well with short-term thinking. It's time to break out of short-term thinking, short-term leadership, and reactionary management. The turbulence caused by the intensifying impact of trends will throw everyone off-balance. Short-term thinkers will be consumed with trying to maintain balance. Long-term thinkers will put day-to-day tremors in perspective as they look at long-term directions and processes.

The enlightened leaders who look more intently—and carefully—toward the future will make better short-term decisions because they can see—and understand—the big picture. They'll be "big thinkers," not "little thinkers."

"Change is here to stay." Everybody knows that. The phrase has been repeated in corporate boardrooms, in college classrooms, in coffee shops, on talk shows, and in convention meeting rooms. Amazingly, even with all this talk, most people are reluctant to change. "Status Quo Forever!," they exclaim. They're so busy exclaiming, they don't see the rest of the world passing them by.

Unfortunately for them, "Change is occurring at an ever-increasing rate." There's another gold-plated truth! Most people stare zombie-like at the velocity of change—overwhelmed and practically incapacitated. They can't break away from the trance enough to see what's happening around them.

When our leaders fall into this trap—and it's easy to do—they make short-term decisions that are, shall we say, inappropriate. No, let's not mince words. Their decisions are downright stupid. Before we fault them too badly, let's recognize that they feel they're making good decisions. . . based on the information they have available.

Oops! There's our fallacy! "Based on the information they have available." Aha! If today's leaders had better information about the future, they would make wiser decisions today. Bingo!

Now what? Well, it seems simple enough. Learn more about the future to understand the turbulence that surrounds us today. Equipped with better knowledge, you will stop making "inappropriate" (read: "stupid") decisions. Think, plan, take action based on long-term thinking.

OK, we've all made some mistakes during the past five years or so. Everything was changing around us; we didn't know what to think! It seemed to make sense to lay off some of our best people-it saved the company a lot of money during tough times. But now, when we need the talent and expertise of those employees, they don't want to return. And finding suitable replacements is increasingly difficult.

Many of us are still trying to run our companies from our thrones in our plush corner offices. Our front-line employees have great ideas, but we can't hear them. We're not close to those people, and our fine middle managers act as an impervious filter to "protect us." Hmmm, we've allowed our middle managers to use our vast resources to. . . well, manage the middle. And they do a fine job managing the middle, protecting it from all encroachments from top, bottom, or outside.

Hint: if you flatten your organizational chart, you and your action-level people get closer together. And you don't need all those excess middle managers, because you no longer have so much middle to be managed. Caveat: Keep your middle managers if they do things that clearly impact your bottom line in a positive way. If they aren't supporting your objectives of earning a profit, operating efficiently, etc., why keep them on the payroll?

By the power vested in me as the author of this book, I hereby grant you absolution for all those "inappropriate" decisions. You are forgiven for all mistakes made through yesterday. Today is a new day—the first day of all that remain. Today you can start doing things more wisely—with greater vision. Today you can begin making a positive difference for yourself and others.

We are moving into an era of intensifying turbulence—the very foundations of what we believe will be shaken. This admonition means we had better start believing more strongly in ourselves. Build new foundations from knowledge and wise, enlightened decisions.

Forget all those things you believed in the past. The future will be considerably different than the past. The future will be significantly different from the present. Get out of your short-term thinking rut and look at what the future holds for you. Understand the trends, appreciate what they will mean in your life—then take action.

Learn about vital trends and watch them evolve. Armed with new insight, you will be able to better manage yourself and your organization. Pay close attention to what seems to be happening and what will probably happen as the years pass. Think about how trends will interact to affect your life. Few individuals are fully cognizant of how trends impact on their lives, so paying attention and acting on this newly acquired information will give you a decided advantage.

As you move through the pages of this book, you'll learn about eleven significant trends that will affect our work environment. While these are certainly not the *only* trends that will impact how work is done, they are the trends that I feel are most significant. My judgments are based on my perspectives as a business futurist concentrating on workforce and workplace issues. These views are strengthened by what I see in the real world in my capacity as a management consultant.

Most of the trends we'll explore are discussed frequently in magazine and newspaper articles, on radio talk shows, and on television news journals. Yet, even with all this coverage, most people, individuals and business leaders alike, seem oblivious to these concerns.

The eleven key trends I have selected are:

1. Economy Heating Up

2. Increasing Use of Technology

3. Demand for Value, Quality and Service

4. Tightening Organizational Structures

5. Corporate Cocooning

6. Shifting Worker Attitudes

7. High Productivity/High Stress

8. Changing Leadership Styles

9. Changing Work Environment

10. Reverse Apprenticeships

11. Self-Control Over Career Destiny

Each of these trends will affect the world of work over the next 15 years. As we'll discuss, some of the activities and events of the past few years have made us more vulnerable. . . and have actually contributed to some of these trends.

Studying trends implies looking into the future. This future insight consumes the energy of a growing body of professionals called futurists. The work of these researchers and forecasters is performed scientifically, without use of crystal balls or tarot cards. Watching trends, futurists can predict with a fair degree of accuracy what will happen in the years ahead.

For generations, we have been fascinated by the future. What will happen to us in the years ahead? How will our lives be different? What will we accomplish? What will we become?

Those of us engaged in managing businesses, government agencies, educational institutions, or not-for-profits, have concentrated on the futures of our organizations. Whether the organization employs one person or thousands, we feel responsible in some way for our employees, our followers.

We read, listen, and watch an assortment of media for information and perspectives about the future. Our research, regardless of how sophisticated it may be, guides us to take certain actions in our lives. These may be actions to respond to relatively immediate situations, or they may be more focused on positioning ourselves for opportunities that may open to us in the years ahead.

Much of what we do is oriented toward our anticipated future circumstances. We consciously prepare ourselves for good experiences. . . and/or protect ourselves from not-so-good experiences. Education is a clear example: we deliberately learn worthwhile knowledge to put ourselves in a position to have more choices, better lives.

Opening new company facilities such as manufacturing plants, distribution centers, and retail outlets, is done for similar reasons. We humans like to build stronger future potential for ourselves. It's a natural phenomenon.

Trends

As we strive to understand the future, it is important to grasp how the future is created. General directions or movements—called "trends"—change and influence what will happen as society evolves.

Some trends are relatively short-lived. We often call them "fads. Sometimes a series of fads establishes a trend. When we use the word "trend," we'll be talking about a series of events, circumstances, perceptions, or habits that are definable, observable and, in many cases very measurable.

Many trends are identified using statistics or research data—even anecdotal evidence. We watch for patterns, or changes in patterns, that suggest what may happen as time passes. Initially, identification of trends and prediction of possible scenarios can be relatively subjective. However, with those hypotheses in mind, futurists can engage in research efforts to substantiate (or repudiate) what they or others envision.

Trends can be sensed in practically any field or situation. The process of visioning is supported by learning and understanding past events and their impacts. Our capacity to envision the future involves a strong grasp of current conditions— regarding the core trend or circumstance, as well as a wide range of related trends and influencing factors.

The stronger your foundation of facts and insights, the easier it is to distinguish legitimate, realistic trends and make viable predictions about where the trends might be taking us.

Impact of Trends

As events follow trends, our lives are influenced by what happens around us. Each trend affects us in some way, directly or indirectly. Sometimes that indirect effect is difficult to see or even accept. Some trends are so remote, we don't ever think about them. Yet, in some small way, through long chains of cause-and-effect, our lives are changed.

Most trends with which we are familiar have a relatively strong impact on who we are and what we do—now and into the future, because they are more meaningful to us. We are more interested in these trends, once we become aware of them, and have greater understanding of their meanings and their implications for our lives.

Many of the events that happen around us, experiences that are part of our lives, can be described as trends. Consider what has happened in your life, and how each of those events, or series of events, supported, impeded, or substantially altered your progress along the path of life.

We manage our lives on the basis of learnings and assumptions. Much of our learnings—teachings, experiences, comes from our growing-up years. Even though we learn quite a bit as adults, our foundation comes from those early years.

As we establish who we are, how we value principles and possessions, what's really important to us, we become understandably set in our ways. We drive stakes into the ground, drop anchors, and mark trees or paths (depending on where we grew up) to build a sense of security and stability for ourselves.

Often we are not aware of trends to any great extent. We simply don't pay much attention to them. Many of us just concentrate on managing our lives in the short-term, investing little energy into much forward thinking and planning. We do what seems appropriate at the time, based on our socialization and experiences, without considering what outside influences might be guiding who we are and what we will become.

Trends impact us whether we're looking in their direction or not. They may even change the opportunities we think are available for us. Trends affect the relative strength of those things we believe in, value, put our stock in. This phenomenon is described by some as climbing the ladder of success, only to find it was leaning against the wrong wall.

If we are not sensitive to—and responsive to—changes in our present and future lives, we may be condemned to continue as we have in the past. Our track to run on can become our rut to get stuck in.

Consider the influence of trends on the value of your education, regardless of what sort of education you've gained. How much of your education were you able to use when you began your career? As your career evolved, how much of what you learned in your formal schooling still applied? As work and career trends continue to influence your job options and choices, how valuable is your formal education as a strength to sell yourself to a prospective employer?

Staying with job and career trends in your chosen field, what different kinds of work will be available to you in the years ahead? How will your work be done differently? What technologies will be used—technologies that may not even exist today? How adaptable are you compared to others who may also want the jobs you desire? How might you have designed your career path differently, if you had a greater understanding of the trends that affect your field? What might you be engaged in today, instead of what you are currently doing?

The impacts of trends can change our lives—often dramatically. If we ignore these trends, life (opportunities) can pass us by. As we shift under the influence of trends, so do our relationships with our loved ones, friends, and surroundings.

Multiple Trend Implications

Our lives are not so simple as to be influenced only by one or two trends. Hundreds, if not thousands, of trends affect our lives every day. Each trend, by itself, has some sort of effect on us—

particularly those that are intertwined with our personal or working lives.

The complications, and the excitement, come with the interaction of trends. Almost every trend has the power to influence other trends. As the trends interconnect, their power becomes even stronger and more far-reaching.

Local trends, national trends, even global trends now influence and modify each other. This interconnection itself is a trend, emphasizing how much our lives can be affected by events or trends that originate halfway around the world.

There are really two different approaches to considering how we are affected by multiple trends. One is to consider each influencing trend on its own merits, exploring how we are affected by each trend individually. The other approach is to recognize how the trends interact with each other to create the eventual impact on our lives.

Together we will explore eleven major trends that will influence our work environment in the near future. Trends influencing the composition and capacity of our workforce will certainly interact with trends about the way work will be done. They influence each other. Technological trends will affect where and how people work and communicate with each other. Those relationship trends will interlink with trends about management and leadership styles.

As you analyze how trends will affect your life, now and into the future, pay close attention to interrelationships between and among trends. Expand your thinking to see yourself interacting differently with your environment.

Some people envision themselves standing on a flat surface, like a street, while trends approach in a linear fashion like an oncoming car. Change your perspective to imagine yourself suspended in open space while trends come at you from virtually all directions.

Knowledge is Power

As you learn about trends that influence your life, you will gain amazing power over your circumstances. You will gain the power to look at yourself differently than you have in the past. You'll be able to take a third person, almost objective, perspective on your present and future.

As you observe the ongoing and changing patterns of trends that affect your life, you'll eventually be able to make some comfortable predictions. Using a process that integrates intuition with factual understandings, you will gain a visionary sense that enables you to "see" things others don't.

Your new-found knowledge, as it develops, will enrich your life. Gradually, you will gain a different sense of control over who you are, what you will do, and who you will become.

We're not talking about being a psychic or journeying flamboyantly "Back to the Future." The experience and insight are very practical and down-to-earth. Anyone can do it. Your advantage is that most people don't.

Find others with whom to discuss your perspectives, insights, and visions. If you really get interested in this sort of forward thinking, you might want to join the World Future Society. You'll enjoy reading the monthly issues of **The Futurist** and perhaps attending the annual conferences of the broad-based eclectic membership. The society's address is Suite 450, 7910 Woodmont Avenue, Bethesda, Maryland 20814. The society's telephone number is (301) 656-8274.

As you share your thoughts with others, you'll hear some different perspectives. Listen carefully to what others have to say. You may pick up one small strand of thinking that could help you understand your circumstances and perspectives even better. You might even modify or harden some of your beliefs based on what you hear from others.

You Control Your Own Destiny

More than ever before, you have control over the destiny of your personal life, your career, and the businesses with which you are involved. With the volume and quality of information available today, on a global scale, you have far greater capacity to determine your own path than any of your ancestors.

Certainly, you may find obstacles blocking your way to achieve what you really want in life. However, with your amplified sense of who you are and what's happening around you, you'll be able to circumvent many of those barriers—and if not circumvent them, at least handle them better.

Knowing what the future may bring, you can prepare more intelligently now to position yourself for the years ahead. You may enlarge your capabilities, change your career path, or take steps to protect yourself (and your company) from any trend-induced calamities that threaten your future success.

Merely feeling that you have gained this stronger sense of control over your life will generate a new aura of confidence. This faith and self-reliance will put you in a wonderful new "space" and will itself suggest new vistas for you. As you open yourself to the myriad of possibilities, you may actually begin to attract opportunities or paths you had not even dreamed of in the past.

Even with all this insight, little will happen until you initiate some changes in your life. You need to take advantage of trend knowledge. Power comes from the practical application of learning, not merely the acquisition of new knowledge.

Gaining the power of insight, then not doing anything to improve your performance, your strength, places you in a rather difficult dilemma. When events that you could see coming from your trend studies start happening, and you become a victim of your circumstances, you will have only yourself to blame. As the old adage goes, "to know and not do is not to know at all."

Use your knowledge and insight about future trends to make a difference in your life and the lives of others. Take steps to gain new skills, new strength to take advantage of emerging opportunities. Protect yourself against your vulnerabilities so you'll be strong enough to survive—to thrive—in the years ahead.

Section 1
Trends

2

Trend
Economy
Heating Up

The economic outlook is different from what many people believe. The economy is heating up, and this will create some fascinating opportunities—and challenges—for all of us. The boom will stimulate and threaten; only the strong will survive. Companies that are not prepared to respond to the increased demand will be at risk!

The economy is almost always a point of discussion when people get together to talk about the future. Everyone seems to have an opinion about how healthy the economy will be, locally, nationally, and globally. And we almost make a sport of finding fault with anyone who predicts changes in the economy. . . or how it should/can be manipulated.

There are practically as many views of the economic future as there are economists talking about it. Let's simplify the issue by suggesting that there are essentially two schools of thought:

1. "The economy is in terrible shape. It will get a lot worse before it gets better. Any trade agreement we make will hurt us. You can't trust the banks. Bury your money in the backyard and wait. Chicken Little was right! The sky is falling!!"

2. "The future is bright. We're not creeping out of the recession; we're roaring out into a strong boom period. Globalization of trade will be a wonderful improvement for everyone. There are all sorts of wonderful investment opportunities. Expect there to be plenty of business for everyone."

From my observations as a futurist, I agree with the second scenario. I see a lot of positive signs; I'll share some with you in a moment.

First, let me pause here for a parenthetical comment. In many of the presentations I make as a professional speaker, I ask my audiences for a show of hands of how many think the economy is in good shape. Very few hands go up in audiences comprised of business owners and executives. On the other hand, about 80% of the hands in groups of sales and marketing audiences are raised— enthusiastically.

What's going on here? Are the sales and marketing folks just optimistic, looking at the world through rose-colored glasses? Or, being closer to where the action is, do they see something their bosses don't see?

Executives do see a broader picture than sales and marketing people do, and they listen to what they hear from others. When enough people grouse about problems in their particular areas, executives naturally hear the negatives. And, since people seem to like to complain about something, that negative feeling can creep into executives' thinking. When your job is to solve problems, the darker the picture, the more secure your job.

Amazingly, most people seem lulled into lethargy about the economy because of what they read in the papers, hear on the radio, or watch on television. Along with the murders, disasters, political shenanigans, and missing children, the reporters test our intelligence by telling us some more bad news about the economy. "Bad news sells," the media people tell us. We want to hear—and believe—the bad stuff.

The recession has been over for quite a while. We're in a growth mode. Economic measurements have gotten stronger with each successive quarter since the early 1990s. "The recession is over! Let it go! Let's move on," I exhort my audiences!

I subscribe to the perspective that the economy is heating up—and quickly. A leading exponent of this philosophy is my colleague, economist/futurist Harry S. Dent, Jr. Harry is the author of *The Great Boom Ahead* (Hyperion Books). This book is a highly readable insight into why the economy will do much better than most people believe.

Harry goes much further than to suggest that the economy will just warm up a little bit. He says we're in a boom period already. His prediction is that we'll see the real evidence starting in the mid 1990s and extending until about 2007. (At that point he expects the Dow to be at 8500). Harry also expects a serious dip at that point from 2008-2022, perhaps the next Great Depression.

I encourage people to read *The Great Boom Ahead* and, if they're interested in current insights from Harry Dent, to subscribe to his informative newsletter, "H. S. Dent Forecast." Call (415) 572-2879. The annual subscription cost is only $98.

What's behind economic growth? It's not the bond market or interest rates. These things are more symptoms than causes. The driving force is consumer spending.

When people buy things, someone has to sell them, someone has to distribute them, and someone has to manufacture them. The more people buy, the stronger the economy. And with improved communication technologies that support faster re-stocking of retail shelves, the lag time between purchase and manufacture has been dramatically shortened.

Consumers typically buy different packages of goods and services at different times in their lives. When they're young and single, or newly married, consumers buy particular kinds of goods and services. As they start families, having children around the house changes the make-up of that package of goods and services. Identifiable changes continue to occur right on through retirement.

Harry Dent's research indicates that spending peaks around age 46, particularly on durable goods like houses, furniture and furnishings, and automobiles. There's a similar peak on his spending wave around age 25 as young people buy durable goods to establish their households.

It stands to reason that the more people we have around age 46 and/or age 25, the stronger our economy will be. Dent found a strong correlation to this hypothesis when he looked comparatively at historical economic cycles.

The first wave of the Baby Boomers is now in its mid to late forties. These folks have lots of money to spend and, watching the statistical trends, they're spending it on durable goods. Many durables manufacturers are wrestling with serious backlogs of orders to fill. They face frustrating problems: the business is there for them, but they can't attract enough qualified employees to work.

The population surge of 25-year olds is secondarily fueling the same market for durable goods. The average age for marrying has risen to 24 for women and 26 for men, a significant increase from a few years ago. People are marrying later, if at all. Single households as well as married households are being established, often by multiple wage-earners who have the income to keep fueling the boom.

When you lay the birth rates of the 76.4 million Baby Boomers against the calendar, it's apparent that millions of people will be reaching age 46 over the next 15 years. The growth will continue. Dent alerts us to his prediction that the greatest effects of the economic boom will be felt from 1997 to 2007.

So, where does the turbulence come from? Retailers must have knowledgeable employees to serve these demanding consumers. Given the very busy schedules of these buyers, they have precious little patience for retail employee incompetence or substandard service. There's plenty of competition for practically any store they shop, and they have no hesitation about going around the corner, down the street, across town, or looking in a catalog to find what they want.

This very lack of good retail help has contributed to the growth of catalog purchasing. Competition will intensify, and the stores or catalogs with the greatest employee knowledge, loyalty, and positive service attitudes will win.

Retailers straining to maximize return on every square foot of floor space will expect reliable, just-in-time delivery from distribution centers. The last thing they want to hear is an excuse. Without merchandise on the shelves, the retailers lose money, as well as customers who might have become loyal, repeat buyers.

Distributors are screaming at manufacturers for high quality merchandise. . . delivered just in time to their warehouses. Transportation companies will be expected to perform much more responsively. Shorter delivery times will become a standard, pushing even more the demand for changes in the ways we all do business.

Some employers will do very well during this exciting era. Others will continue holding fast to old style plans and procedures that worked fine 20, 10, 5, or just 3 years ago. The slower they are to change, the greater the potential for more flexible and fast-moving companies to eat away at their market share.

Is strong economic growth good news for your company? It sounds great, on the surface. But, can you handle a two or three-fold increase in business with little time to prepare? Companies that invest time and other resources into improving their systems and training their people will be much better prepared for the opportunities. Companies that don't concentrate on preparing now may find themselves overwhelmed, with potentially serious consequences including shut-down.

Shut down? Yes, companies can be forced to close their doors because of too much business. There is a natural tendency (call it "greed") to accept every order you can. This practice leads to over-promising and, consequently, under-delivering. Under-served customers become discontented and take their business elsewhere. Employees who don't like the push-push pressure will leave to seek more orderly work environments. Few orders, fewer employees: shut-down.

Earlier, I mentioned some trends I watch as economic indicators of sorts. I promised to share these perspectives with you:

1. Manufacturers have sizable backlogs of orders in a number of industries.

2. Executive search firms report a notable increase in requests for senior level executives and managers.

3. Those companies which produce equipment used in manufacturing have seen strong increases in business, to the extent that they have had difficulty keeping up.

These, and other indicators, suggest that a much stronger economy is close-at-hand, regardless of what happens in Washington. The expanding economy will create significant turbulence for employers who are not ready for the impacts. Many will be caught unaware and will suffer from loss of business as demanding customers go to more adaptive competitors. They also stand to lose valued employees who will be stolen by more aggressive employers.

This expanding economy will stimulate the development of new technologies. Growing companies will want to take advantage of every technology they can. . . but applying these new technologies won't be as simple as you might think. The next chapter tells the story.

3

Trend

Increasing
Use of
Technology

The rapid introduction of new technologies will alternately frighten and inspire employers and workers. Training costs and resistance to change will overwhelm many employers, and the precarious balance between man and technology will be threatened, disrupting the workplace.

In an effort to increase productivity—output per hours worked, employers are finding new ways to use technology to reduce human work hours. A primary objective is to replace human capital with technological capital, protecting the employer against the uncertainty of changes in employment regulations, healthcare programs, and taxation.

Of course, only a small percentage of new technologies ever directly displaces workers. And new positions are often created to support new systems. More often, technology is introduced to help workers accomplish more, do their work more efficiently or more accurately, or do it in a more manageable way.

With the drive for higher productivity in the workplace, many executives believe the application of new technologies will be a panacea. Not so. Technologies, especially those approaches they don't really understand, hold a certain "snake oil" magic for these executives. Such thinking actually blocks the proper introduction of appropriate technological advances. A powerful technology applied to antiquated or ill-conceived procedures will merely do the same bad job faster, not better.

We can expect to experience some dramatic changes as a result of the introduction of new technology, and further application of existing and advanced technology. This process will be exciting for some, threatening for others. In some cases, new technology will be welcomed enthusiastically. In other situations, we'll see sabotage employed in an effort to slow the intimidating drive into the future.

It is impossible to address the wide range of developing technologies in this book. To be relevant to workforce and workplace issues, I've chosen to concentrate on technologies that will have the most direct effect on the most people in their work. For some exciting insights into technology and its application, I suggest you read *Technotrends* by my colleague, Dr. Dan Burrus. It was published by HarperBusiness.

Computers have become an integral part of corporate America. We've gone from mainframes to desktop personal computers. Now laptops and notebook computers are commonplace, and palm-sized computers are gaining in popularity. The technology exists for powerful computers that will hook on your belt, be carried in your purse, or even worn on your wrist. The Dick Tracy communications fantasy of comic strip fame is now reality.

Cellular communications technology, modems, electronic mail, and the Internet are all alive, well, and getting more powerful. Even with all the talk about the "information highway," though, most people are nervous about even looking for the on-ramp.

These technologies will have an increasing impact on the way we work. With enhanced communications capability, relationships between companies, departments, and individuals have been changed forever. Accelerated communications systems such as electronic data interchange (EDI) and even broadcast facsimiles have all but eliminated time delays in information transfer.

The infusion of communications technology will continue to change how—and where—people work. Many workers won't have to go into the office anymore; they'll be able to work from home or even from someone else's home while on a mini-vacation. They'll enjoy a new freedom of being able to work almost anywhere and anytime.

This advantage over site-based workers may engender jealousy between positions that could cause relationship and labor problems in the future. Employers who seek to avoid competitive internal conflict may introduce different kinds of technology for each employee, fostering a sense of inclusion—of team involvement.

One of my clients on the east coast, an engineering firm, was about to lose a valued design engineer. His parents were ailing and he had decided to move back to the farm in Nebraska to take care of them. Not wanting to lose his valuable talents, the employer funded a work station for this employee—in his parents' farmhouse. The engineer works at his computer, completely connected electronically with the firm's office on the east coast. It's a virtual workspace, a transparent, seamless connection—clients and colleagues interact with him almost as if he were in the office down the hall.

A trade association manager and her husband decided to yield to a yearning to move to the community of their dreams, Louisville, Kentucky. Instead of giving up her beloved job in the Washington, D.C. area, she uses technology to operate quite efficiently from her remote office in Louisville.

For many workers, physical location is becoming less important. American firms experiencing a shortage of employees with software engineering skills meet their needs using talented people from other countries. Indian, Philippine, and Irish engineers can be hired on a contract basis at 25% to 40% of the cost of comparable in-country workers. . . and they'll do business across high-speed data lines. No travel or relocation expenses.

Technology and common sense will be applied in a wide range of settings to increase efficiency and reduce costs. Communications technology will be the most visible, since it will be used by the most people.

Manufacturing foremen, often hard to reach through loud speakers that distract everyone in the plant, now use pagers and cellular phones to respond to calls. When they need support on the floor, they use the phone in their pocket instead of wasting time walking across the area to the closest wired phone.

We're just touching the surface in this brief exploration of technology. Picture phones are right around the corner, as are other improvements that are still on the drawing boards. Research and introduction times have been drastically shortened, so we can expect to see a wide range of new products being introduced rather quickly.

Capital equipment manufacturers are upgrading their products—to stay abreast (or ahead) of the competition. They are already behind with a frustrating backlog of orders, with customers asking for upgrades to improve their own productivity. This pattern will continue for the next 10-15 years, at least as rapid changes in technology stimulate new generations of tools and equipment. What workers learn how to operate today will be obsolete tomorrow. . . and "tomorrow" is coming faster and faster.

Need for Training

The increasing application of technology places demands on employees to learn new methods and systems. . . and to unlearn the habits and techniques they've used so comfortably in the past. Most workers—at all levels and across industry lines, must undergo some dramatic shifts in the way they perform their responsibilities. Sharp, or at least constantly climbing, learning curves will become a way of life.

Employees will have to learn new skills continuously to maintain their effectiveness. This truth applies to front line technicians, senior executives, and everyone in between. Even sales professionals will be affected. The American Society for Training and Development estimates that 75% of our workforce must be retrained before the turn of the century. That's a major challenge!

And training itself has undergone some significant technological changes. In some organizations, on-the-job training has been replaced by interactive video and training programs on CD-ROM. Seminars are led by instructors who have had to become proficient in the use of educational and presentation software like Microsoft's PowerPoint®.

For some adult learners, the process of gaining knowledge and skills is intimidating. They are not comfortable using computers; their lack of understanding of the technology makes operating a computer a frightening experience. This fear blocks their ability to effectively take advantage of training that is done by computer. It's another obstacle in the retraining process.

However it is accomplished, the re-training of the workforce is essential. And it will be expensive—in terms of designing the technology to do the training, people to conduct the training programs, and the time of the people who need to be retrained.

The cost of designing and delivering this training must be borne by the corporate community.

As that realization has evolved, executives have protested loudly. Few businesses believe they should have the responsibility of training their workers in every aspect of their jobs. They prefer that workers have an abundance of training before being hired—that they should bring this level of preparation with them.

Employers are reluctant. . . resistant. . . to the idea that they should pay for extensive training. Training costs can take a substantial amount of money right off the bottom line. As expensive as training and development can be, wise employers will nevertheless invest in quite a bit of it for their people. Paying for learning will still be the most cost-effective way for employers to be sure their people have the knowledge and skills to get the job done.

Understandably, these employers will be more demanding of workers who become trained at their expense. The great fear is that they'll expend all these resources to train people. . . who will then leave to join another employer. Yet in reality, employees appreciate training and can be expected to show that appreciation by staying around for a while.

One vision of this training concern is that employees will continually acquire knowledge and skills, working for employers who train them as part of the employment agreement. These more proficient employees repay the employer with a higher quality of performance before moving on to another employment opportunity. . . where they will acquire another dose of training and development. They will be succeeded by other transient employees with background and experience to make a contribution to corporate success in return for their growth. And the cycle continues, utilizing this resilient workforce as part of the big picture of future employment relationships.

Employers will seek workers who are already trained, ready to go to work. The message to prospective employees is clear: get extensive training and education on your own to make yourself more attractive to the companies you want to work for. If already employed by a company you want to stay with, volunteer for learning opportunities whenever they become available. Demonstrate a desire to learn and grow.

Older employees are often intimidated by new technology—and by younger employees who have learned about the new methods in school. A "techno-chasm" can form, creating an uncomfortable (and counter-productive) gap between employees with very different technological competencies.

The technologically-prepared employees may be seen as a threat by those with more traditional experience and training. Low-tech employees, though quite competent in their fields, may feel that they don't "fit" anymore. They may encounter difficulties communicating and making viable contributions. These feelings sometimes cause valued employees to leave an organization, in search of a more comfortable, less technological, and perhaps less demanding, work environment.

In his writings, futurist John Naisbitt addresses the importance of the sensitive relationship between technology and people. He describes the need as a balance between high tech and high touch. This balance, once established, must be carefully maintained. People and technology serve each other. It's a delicate relationship. If more weight is put on one, at the unconsidered expense of the other, problems will ensue.

Technology is developing rapidly—and change is occurring at an ever-accelerating pace— so much that people easily become disoriented. New technology should be introduced in ways that make it comfortable for those who will use it. . . and for those who will eventually benefit from it. The balance between technology and humans must be carefully nurtured through each step of the process.

Because technologies have often been shoved into place in some organizations, there is a strong undercurrent of resistance to new methods and new systems. Wise employers assure that people are truly comfortable with existing technology and agree with the need for something else. . . *before* introducing any new technology.

We've seen a tendency to rush technologies into place without providing enough training for people to use them well. This training is essential and, if skipped or glossed over, can cripple aggressive employers.

Training and re-training needs are tremendous. Many companies are ill-prepared for these demands, having gutted their training departments during the down-sizing process. Yes, tradition held: training and advertising were among the first cuts in a lot of companies! It's fascinating to watch cost-sensitive companies cut those costs that can build sales and productivity.

Enlightened employers are scrambling to find internal and external resources to train and educate employees—front line operators, supervisors, managers, salespeople, and even executives. Changes in leadership styles, work group organization and management, interpersonal relationships and roles all need the support of qualified instructors and change facilitators.

With this perspective, it's easy to predict an increasing demand for experienced training professionals in the corporate world. Trainers with expertise in current and emerging technologies will be especially sought.

Peter Senge in his book, *The Fifth Discipline*, described how companies must become "learning organizations." The very culture of leading companies will include an emphasis on continual learning and professional growth.

I agree strongly with this perspective. "Learning" organizations have a much better chance of becoming strong "earning" organizations. The technologies to be learned are certainly not limited to computers, electronics, or robotics. The way we interact with each other, the way we build relationships with our customers, the way we distribute our products and services can all be described as technologies in the broader sense.

Exposing the "Big Picture"

Most employees have some sense for what goes on in their area of the company, but that's as far as their knowledge goes. They have very little understanding of what happens in adjacent departments or in process-connected functional areas. Appreciation of what the entire company is doing is rare. We have had a tendency not to show people the "big picture."

The "big picture" perspective has been reserved for people at the upper levels of the corporate hierarchy. The trend in this area is shifting to bringing more people into big picture enlightenment. This greater understanding is essential for the empowerment process to work to its full potential.

When employees understand the company's full objectives, those employees are able to laser-focus their energies to help achieve those objectives. The trend among astute employers appears to be a strong emphasis on sharing big picture perspectives and enhanced cross-functional communication.

The trend is first seen during the new employee orientation process. Instead of just taking new workers to their assignments, introducing them to their supervisors, and showing them where the restores are, a more comprehensive approach is being used in enlightened work environments.

New hires are given a big picture look at what the company is and does. The orientation often begins with an explanation of the company's mission, values, vision, and goals. The organizational structure is introduced, pointing out where the new person fits and emphasizing the collaborative interplay between and among departments and functions.

Tours of the company help the new employee see what the place looks like, who the people are, and how work flows through to completion. This design for orientation builds a greater sense of belonging and personal responsibility to fellow workers. There's an increasing amount of discussion about seeing employees as internal customers.

I've seen some companies do a beautiful job of bringing new people on board. Surprisingly, some of them have forgotten to take the existing employees through the same process. Assuming that current employees already know what is covered in orientation is a dangerous trap.

If you neglect current employees and fuss over new hires, your loyal producers will become alienated. The messages they send new hires, as they work side-by-side, may not be congruent with what the new folks have just been taught. Companies that don't assure that everyone is "singing from the same sheet of music" will soon detect a lack of harmony.

Perspective

Even though rapidly changing technology will cause substantial turbulence, the more serious problem will be the human element. There is no question that we'll experience increasingly rapid change fueled by new technologies replacing the "old." We've seen this already; the insight is that this challenging process will intensify. Expect to see shake-up. . . and shake-out as companies (or their people) fail to keep up.

Worker comfort with change, learning, total organization immersion, and high tech/high touch balance will be determining factors of success. Demands placed by customers will be passed along to employees. The further down the system we go, the more difficulty may be incurred.

Blockages will be seen at mid-manager levels; they'll be too far from the action and will be confused by new technology. Charges of blocking information flow have been thrown at managers for years. This phenomenon is about to take on a whole information flow have been thrown at managers for years. This phenomenon is about to take on a whole new meaning. Managers who don't roll up their sleeves and work more closely with their teams will find themselves extinct. The refusal, inability, or failure to communicate and collaborate with the rest of the team will become a fatal offense.

But whether confronted by high tech or high touch, the challenges of the future will demand a different kind of performance. Technology will have its place, but managers and their employees will also have to provide new levels of quality, value, and service. The byword may be something like "deliver or die" as companies are forced to produce . . . or go out of business.

4

Trend
Demand for Value, Quality, and Service

Rising consumer demand for value, quality, and service will severely challenge many companies. Competition for customers will intensify, raising performance expectations. Some companies will fail in this race—unable to provide sufficient levels of value, quality, and service because they lack competent, trained and dedicated employees who can perform for their customers.

Building on the consumerism movement that surfaced in the 1970s, customers want more from their suppliers. There are increasing demands for quality merchandise and higher levels of service— before, during, and after the sale. If customers don't get what they want, they'll abandon the supplier for one that will meet their expectations.

Increasing demands by consumers on their retailers have a ripple effect that takes the higher expectations right back to manufacturers and suppliers of raw materials. Customers at all levels of the supply chain demand more, and will happily take their business elsewhere if they don't get what they want.

Customer loyalties to suppliers are much different than they have been in the past. In the years ahead, we can expect customers to become even more particular. They will insist on high value for the dollars they spend and their perception of value will include numerous aspects of their purchase:

- quality of the product or service
- availability of merchandise for delivery
- delivery system—speed, access, accuracy, responsiveness
- pricing policies, options, flexibility
- knowledge and helpfulness of employees, attitude and availability

- communications mechanisms—before, during, and after the sales/delivery process (application of technologies as Electronic Data Interchange and e-mail)
- terms of payment
- partnering and strategic alliances.

As competing suppliers match each other's offerings, more aggressive suppliers will look for ways to add value to their relationships with their customers. The dynamic creativity stimulated by intensifying competition will keep more traditional suppliers off-balance until they change their strategies.

Some purchasers are negotiating sole supplier agreements to give them more bargaining power for quality, delivery, pricing, and overall responsiveness. Others have consciously decided to deal with several competing suppliers to keep everyone striving eagerly to earn the purchasers' business.

What all purchasers seem to say, at all levels, is that they are prepared to shift their business to competitors if their preferred supplier doesn't perform. They expect their supplier(s) to have competent, knowledgeable employees who can answer questions and get the job done. When this support isn't there to a sufficient degree, they'll be gone in the blink of an eye.

Taking the lead from the philosophy of Total Quality Management, emphasis is placed on serving customers. These customers want results, not just smiles and platitudes. If they're not satisfied (or "delighted," if you want to use the current vernacular), they'll take their business to a competitor.

Some employers have taken the bold move of giving managers the power to seek vendors outside of the company if internal sources don't meet their needs. Normally secure bureaucratic departments are being shaken to their foundations by the need to compete and perform for the right to continue to exist within their parent organizations.

It takes qualified, experienced, dedicated people to meet customer demands. The strongest response comes from stable organizations comprised of people who know what they're doing. They know their customers, their product or service, and the delicate history of important relationships. When customers know they can count on the people who work for a supplier, the level of confidence and loyalty is much higher.

Total Quality Management: Fad or Trend?

The industry-wide push for Total Quality Management (or Continuous Quality Improvement—choose your terminology) has met with mixed results. After a flurry of interest for several years, the Baldrige Quality Award program is attracting fewer entries.

Our firm's informal research estimates that about 80% of attempts at Total Quality fail, usually because the organizational culture is not ready to support the new performance design. Most companies are simply not prepared for the different systems technology required for Total Quality Management.

When not handled properly, quality initiatives not only fail—they backfire! Workers, who were "burned" or felt failure in the process, will deliberately avoid anything that even smells like a quality program.

Before introducing movements toward improved quality, be sure your corporate culture will sustain and maintain the shift. The supportive culture should genuinely encourage empowerment. Everyone should feel comfortable offering suggestions for improvement, even when they run counter to what has always been done before. Executives should sincerely condone risk-taking, and avoid any temptation to go on "witch hunts" when something fails.

Continuous improvement is here to stay, but I question whether formal Total Quality Management programs will survive. The philosophy is legitimate, but the methodology is not so firmly entrenched. The technology of TQM efforts will be massaged and re-packaged. The result, after the consultants and zealots are shaken out, will be improved work driven by the people who perform it.

The employees of today and tomorrow don't want police watchdogs following their every move. They don't want supervisors looking over their shoulders. Instead, they want to understand the objectives, then manage the process on their own.

Earlier quality initiatives emphasized control, constant checking of finished work to be sure it was right. Inspectors were everywhere and workers felt the heat. When the quality movement shifted the responsibility and accountability to the worker, results improved. Even though it may be uncomfortable at first, workers do want more responsibility and will accept the accountability that goes with it.

Part of the challenge for future organizational leaders will be to find ways to genuinely empower employees to take charge of their own work. We're seeing the beginnings of this shift with the success of self-directed work teams. The key will be to link accountability and authority with the assignment of responsibility, moving away from the practice of simply telling people what to do. Each worker will assume accountability for accomplishment of specific tasks and objectives.

Total Quality Management in the future will become less of a program and more of a teaching mechanism and style of operating. The quality efforts in the future will be focused on thinking and performing, rather than on measuring every little step along the path of production.

The technologies of quality management, along with the technologies managers introduce to try to improve quality, will go through some dramatic changes during the next decade. Continuous improvement efforts will remain—as the clear responsibility of each worker, rather than as formal programs. The customer will be served!

This continuous improvement effort is only one of the ways in which employers are responding to the demands of their customers, making dramatic changes in the way they do business. They're also cutting out fat, slashing bureaucracy, and streamlining operations to move into the future as lean machines. The next chapter explains how this trend may affect you.

5

Trend
Tightening
Organizational
Structures

Employers have begun tightened their organizational structures, aggressively striving to eliminate fat, slack, and redundancy. The old "rules" about hierarchies, entitlements, and appropriate relationships have been declared null and void. It's a whole new ball game as companies turn upside down and inside out. Nothing is sacred.

During the late 1980s, in a period of relative prosperity, many employers "fattened up." Seeing wonderful opportunities in the marketplace, they added people, facilities, equipment, product lines, and other resources. This greed-generated approach was smart for the times. Business was good, and there was little concern for emphasizing efficiencies or placing too much importance on controlling costs.

However, in the early 1990s, after the economy's strength had been waning and we moved into a recession, these employers found themselves with an embarrassing excess of high-cost overhead. Expenses had slipped out of control. As the impacts of the recession hit, employers were overexposed and vulnerable.

Suddenly, the companies that had been so responsive to the marketplace found themselves with an overhead burden that could not be supported by declining sales and revenues. At the same time, their operating costs were increasing. Something had to be done!

Reviewing their available options to tighten expenditures quickly, corporate leaders zeroed in on personnel as a convenient cost-reduction target. With business down, not as many people were needed, so employers felt justified in cutting payroll. At first, the reductions-in-force took the form of layoffs. In most cases, the last to be hired became the first to be let go. This approach was rather traditional and was understood by all concerned.

Some corporate leaders maintained existing take-advantage-of-the-opportunity strategies. They believed that the downturn would be short and relatively uneventful, so they didn't make many changes. Personnel cuts were not as dramatic or deep at the onset of the recession. They had the resources to hold off, and did so in the hopes of being well-positioned to prosper as soon as the short-lived downturn was over. These employers eventually had to bite the same bullet, but their layoffs came later in the recession. News of these personnel cuts prolonged the sense of recessionary despair.

At first, the focus of the cost-cutting remained on reducing the expenses of employing human resources. Early retirement programs were designed and implemented to remove more people from the payroll. This strategy helped companies reduce personnel costs through removal of higher-paid employees. But there was an unexpected serious cost. Many employers inadvertently lost a valuable base of experience, wisdom, and maturity as senior workers took advantage of the high-benefit opportunities to start a new life/career.

The shedding of "redundant" employees continued, often generating high profile news stories when large numbers of people were cut at one time. Employers aggressively reduced the number of positions available to be occupied by current—or future—workers. The largest cuts were in middle management, but many other kinds of jobs were also eliminated or modified in the shedding process.

This employee-reduction exercise saved a lot of companies, but hurt a lot of people. The cuts went so deep in some companies that pink slips were given to people who had been loyal employees for many years. . . even decades. Any remaining sense of corporate loyalty to faithful employees had evaporated.

As economic problems continued, it became evident that more dramatic actions would be needed. While personnel downsizings continued in almost every industry, it obviously wasn't enough. Many corporations were still hurting financially.

Wise corporate leaders, realizing the danger of stripping their companies of too many of their competent employees, began evaluating other methods of controlling their costs. "Downsizing" became "rightsizing" as companies initiated restructuring, rebirth, and reengineering.

Flattening of organizational charts became popular. Whole layers of management were removed, bringing other managers closer to front line workers. On the surface, this initiative appeared the right thing to do, but employers encountered unexpected side effects.

Managers who had concerned themselves with organizational and process issues now were forced to re-connect with operational responsibilities. For many, it was like re-learning a foreign language that had been long forgotten. Computer technology didn't assume as much of the managerial load as flat organization advocates had predicted.

Hourly workers didn't always respond the way theorists anticipated. Even with all the noise about empowerment, non-management employees didn't rush forward to take on new responsibilities. Employers discovered they had done a fine job of training employees to do just what they were told— to the extent that many workers didn't know how to think for themselves. . . or didn't want to. The concept of empowerment frightened managers, too.

If they relinquished their power and direction roles, would their jobs be in jeopardy—would they even be needed anymore? The managers heard talk about playing a different kind of leadership role, but no one was teaching them how to make the transition. Understandably protective of their positions, they resisted true empowerment.

Genuine empowerment can work. Pushing responsibility and accountability to the lowest possible level in an organization is a good thing to do—for the company and for its employees. But before empowerment becomes real, a culture change and some careful training is required. It won't just happen with a wave of a magic wand!

Seeking solutions to the problems created by decades of insufficient leadership, corporate leaders began examining how they actually do business. Reaching back to earlier ideas like zero-based budgeting, employers started redesigning themselves. They challenged every aspect of mission, vision, structure, market, product, process, location—everything. Reengineering became vogue as we sought better ways of doing things. In some cases, eager employers went on reengineering binges without taking time to diagnose where the real problems were.

The transformation that will take place in corporate life will not happen quickly. It's not an overnight process. It must begin with a clear understanding of the principles that form your foundation. Employers of the future will be much more focused on the "why" of doing business. We'll experience more of this search for deeper meeting in the years ahead, but the focus in the immediate future will be on core business, efficiency, and cost control.

"Tightsizing"

The aggressive efforts to reduce costs and improve bottom line profitability shifted employers toward the once-popular theme of operating like a "lean, mean fighting machine." In the 90s, however, it wasn't politically correct to be mean. And "fighting" didn't seem appropriate, even though competition for sales dollars was intensifying.

The "lean" connotation was legitimate. With this new mission in mind, executives now concentrated on reducing costs. In my writing, consulting, and speaking, I described this new trend as "tightsizing."

As the tightsizing trend progressed, executives and board members challenged almost everything their companies did. They examined their corporate structures, management styles, product lines, methods of distribution, systems for accomplishing work, outsourcing versus in-house departments, and any aspect that could be described as "We've always done it that way."

Restructuring usually included elimination of positions, causing many frightened employees to characterize any outside consultant as wielding a hatchet to chop more jobs from the payroll. Employees became suspicious, and consequently less supportive of creative ways to improve bottom line performance.

Citing the enhanced communication and improved management control they achieved through computerization, employers wiped out entire levels of management. So many middle managers were let go, some commentators began describing the economic downturn as "the white collar recession." Many white collar positions were eliminated; but, in fairness, many of those positions were the ones that were created when employers fattened up.

Quality programs were in vogue during this period. An understandable connection was made between initiating Total Quality Management campaigns and eliminating jobs. Quality promotions were seen by cynical workers as a management ploy to cut more jobs. Unfortunately, this tactic really was the motivation for TQM in some companies.

We watched a surge of corporate merger and acquisition activity as efforts were made to streamline operations, eliminate duplication of effort or product, and generate new economies of scale.

New technologies were applied, often before people were prepared to implement them. Things were moving fast and furiously in the world of work. Employees were feeling alienated from their employers and even from the work they were doing. But, the bottom lines were looking better.

The tightsizing trend continues today—and will into the foreseeable future, as corporate leaders watch costs very closely. The tendency to be almost too tight will probably continue beyond its time of necessity in some companies. They'll wonder what happened as more trend-sensitive astute competitors begin aggressively pursuing new markets. Being too tight can be just as dangerous as being too loose.

Impacts of Tightsizing

One of the impacts of the tightsizing trend is the need to depend more on fewer people to get the work done. The people who are employed must be more consistently competent. There is no more room for employees who don't meet the standards, and those standards are deliberately being raised.

The emphasis now among employers is to be more careful in hiring: selecting the best candidates and expecting them to produce at higher levels of productivity. This higher selectivity reduces the number of applicants employers consider to be qualified for employment.

Prospective employees have to strengthen their qualifications and their position pursuit approach to be more attractive to these employers. The dynamics of the process of connecting positions and applicants will change significantly during the balance of the 1990s and even more into the next decade.

Expect recruiting to be much more aggressive...and employees to be much more receptive to inquiries. Employers will raise their hiring standards—the investment in recruiting and the need for really good employees will drive this trend. Employers and employees will negotiate roles, responsibilities, employment period, and professional growth, in addition to compensation and work sites.

The tightening criteria for hiring makes the recruiting process even more difficult. Fewer people in the labor pool will meet the stronger expectations. The lean approach to employment makes each employee more valuable, and often harder to replace.

The increased reliance on fewer people and the implementation of the higher standards, coupled with the reduced numbers of available qualified applicants, creates a dangerous vulnerability for most employers. The loss of any one employee will have a stronger potential negative impact than when there were plenty of extra people to pick up the slack.

Qualified replacements will be harder to recruit and hire, placing employers in a difficult position. They must have competent people to do the work to meet customer expectations. Having an important position go unfilled for any length of time can have serious negative impacts on the organization's performance, threatening long-term relationships with valued customers.

We can no longer just hire "warm bodies" to fill positions. As soon as other employees see that the company's standards have been compromised, their respect for the higher standards of performance will erode.

Another impact of tightsizing will be a sense of agility, of flexibility. The lean companies will have so little fat, they will have the capacity to act more quickly. This strength will enable them to take advantage of emerging opportunities and correct any difficulties that arise.

The application of this capacity is dependent, of course, on having enlightened management with the desire and courage to move swiftly. They'll have to disregard the old conventions and take bold, aggressive actions.

Employees will expect their leaders to make things happen. Reducing the fat is one thing; letting the muscle turn to flab is quite another. Balance between strength and action is important. Corporate fitness will be a wise strategy, but performance will be essential to keep the new "body" in good shape. It's a process that doesn't stop.

Astute leaders will continue to remove the fat from their organizations. They'll concentrate on core business and shed every operation and excess employee they can. The stockholders will be happy with the higher productivity and profit figures, but there's a risk involved.

If companies are too tight, they will lack the resilience necessary to respond quickly to emerging opportunities. Losing just one valued employee could be devastating. Employers may now consider it a luxury to have "extra" people whose job it is to be alert for new opportunities. But, in the fast-moving and turbulent future, investment in such resources will enable employers to be nimble. Windows of opportunity will be small and quick action will essential to compete effectively.

And that exposure leads us to a critical vulnerability which exists in most organizations. Those valued employees are ready to jump ship. They're disgusted, fed-up, and disillusioned, all of which means preparing your organization for its future may not be as easy as it looks. The next chapter puts a different perspective on the real—or potential—strength of these lean machines.

6

Trend
Corporate
Cocooning

Frustrated employees have been trapped in jobs they didn't want. Their work isn't fun anymore. Workers have not been treated well and they're not happy. Their attitudes have contributed to a strong desire to break out of the traditional world of work and create whole new designs. Their feeling: it's time for change!

During the recession of the early 1990s, fewer jobs were available. Even through the post-recessionary period, opportunities to change jobs were severely limited. Continuing news media stories about layoffs, downsizings, and economic troubles perpetuated the feeling that there just weren't any positions available.

Practically every worker was touched, directly or indirectly, by the recession-inspired personnel cuts. If layoffs, early retirements, and other reductions in force didn't happen in the worker's own company, then probably friends, relatives, or neighbors were victims.

In the face of these economic troubles, most employees elected to stay in their current jobs. In fact, they were very happy to have jobs at all, given the difficulties they heard others experiencing. Employees were simply "clinging" to the jobs they had.

Many of these workers didn't like their work, their employer, their supervisor, their co-workers, the location, the pay, and/or a variety of other factors. However, seeing no other place to go, they reluctantly stayed where they were.

I call this phenomenon "corporate cocooning" —remaining within the safety and security of an established corporate position, even though you may not want to be there. Corporate cocooners often feel trapped, unable to grow, unable to be what they really want to be.

The longer these employees remain in positions that are uncomfortable for them, the stronger their desire will be to jump the fence to where the grass is greener. They're waiting and watching. When they perceive that the time is right, they'll be psychologically ready to go.

These employees—and they're at all levels in most organizations—are not staying on the job because of loyalty to their employers. They don't express the same loyalty to employers as they did in the past. The perceived ruthless chopping of long-term employees crushed any feelings of loyalty that remained.

If employees don't see any reason to stay, they're ready to leave. They'll be looking, diligently, for new positions. Psychologically, they may be gone—even though you still see the body there. If they feel nothing is holding them to a particular employer, they'll move to what they'll perceive as better positions at the first good opportunity.

Will this moving to better positions be cumulative for employers that have enjoyed low turnover in recent years? It's really hard to say. Thinking about this question reminds me of a recent conversation I had with a troubled manager of a manufacturing plant in New England.

This fellow keeps meticulous records. After he read my book, *Keeping Good People*, he telephoned to pose a question. His employee turnover had been at a steady rate of 15%—until the recession hit and slowed the movement. Turnover dropped to 3.2%. His concern was whether his normal rate would be cumulative! When the recession ended, would the turnover rate increase by 11.8% for the ensuing years—and would it all happen at once?

We know some people will leave. Expect it. Some percentage of turnover is good—to bring in new blood and clean out nonproducers. Turnover will occur even when most employees are choosing to remain in the comfort of the corporate cocoon. People will talk with each other; realize that your people are doing a lot of thinking and talking about their futures—with your company or somewhere else.

Workers now assert that their primary allegiance must be to themselves. No longer can they rely on their employers to take care of them, to protect them against the ravages of economic instability.

In past generations, workers stayed with one company for 10, 20, 30, or 40 years. This norm continued strongly throughout the "Parent Generation"—those born prior to 1946. People who changed jobs more frequently then, say, five years, were described as "job hoppers." The term was not regarded by most as a compliment.

This trend has shifted to changing jobs as frequently as necessary to move forward in their careers. Rapid changes in industry, and the job opportunities that resulted from those developments, enhanced this tendency.

We haven't seen heavy job-jumping for a few years. Some movement has occurred, but more as an undercurrent. Frequent movement hasn't been prevalent, or even noticeable, for several years as the instability and dampening of the recession slowed the process. Now that the recession is over, expect to see less true loyalty and more look-out-for-yourself attitudes and behavior.

The higher frequency job shifting trend was already in place before the recession. The Bureau of Labor Statistics of the United States Department of Labor reported in the early 1990s that the average job tenure was 4.6 years. Workers change jobs 11 times—and change careers more than three times—during their lifetimes.

Given the values we're seeing demonstrated by the Baby Buster Generation (the 68.5 million people born between 1964 and 1985), I predict even greater turnover and shorter tenures. Members of this generation began entering the workforce in 1984 and will continue to enter until about 2005. Their independence says they will *not* conform to the pattern of staying in one position for a long period of time. As their practice of continually moving from job to job becomes accepted, the velocity of the change will probably increase.

The temporary tightening of the labor market has been a counter-trend. This condition means that workers have not stayed in their jobs out of loyalty, but rather out of fear. They haven't felt that they had choices, because they couldn't see or reach better positions. They don't want to be in those corporate cocoons. They want out!

Very few employers have done much to build employee loyalty during the first half of the 1990s. With some notable exceptions, most employers have taken the attitude that there are plenty of people on the unemployment line. With this belief that there is an abundance of qualified employees, they don't expect difficulty replacing people that leave. They act as though it's not necessary to value current employees and strive to keep them. Workers have been regarded as a replaceable commodity.

Some interesting surveys have been taken about worker attitudes over the past few years. An example is the survey conducted by **Industry Week Magazine** and reported in its November 2, 1992 issue. **Industry Week** asked over 500 workers if it was "fun" where they worked. The response was clear: 67% said it was *not* fun to go to work. This proportion is up from 63% who said work wasn't fun when they were surveyed in 1990. The survey was not repeated in 1994.

Exploring who's not having fun, some fascinating insight surfaces from the 1992 data. Vice presidents aren't so happy—61.3% answered "no,." they're not having fun at work. 63.1% of middle managers and 77.6% of first-line supervisors also answered "no." And non-management employees? 74.8% said they're not having fun. Considering what's been happening in the workplace over the past couple of years, I would assume the numbers of dissatisfied workers would be even higher today.

It's not difficult to extrapolate some additional insight from this kind of a survey response. If those workers are not happy—as front line employees, supervisors, managers, or even vice presidents, we can safely assume that they would be receptive to other opportunities. If another employer offered them a position where they felt they could "have fun" in their work, who wouldn't leap to the new job?

My contention is that if these people are not having fun, are not enjoying their work, they'll be even more open to—if not actively looking—for other employment alternatives. And, as the economy heats up, more and more alternatives will be available.

Yes, there still are some people who believe that work should be a drudgery—not at all enjoyable. "Work is work, and fun is fun," they say. But those folks are in the minority. With the wide range of choices of employment available today, people are looking for more than "it's a job" and some money in their pockets. They want more.

So many people, enmeshed in that "corporate cocoon," simply "attend" work. They are present in body, but not in spirit. Psychologically, in many cases, there's nobody there. The "check-your-brains-at-the-door syndrome" is still alive and well in our corporate world.

This attitude is not the way most people want to live. People want to be valued in their work environment. They want to feel that they are worthwhile, that they're making a viable contribution to their employer. When this feeling dissipates, it's time for a change. Today's workers won't tolerate living with a feeling that they're wasting their lives.

A generation or two ago, staying in that corporate cocoon was seen as a good thing. Not any more. They want to climb out of that rut and seek more fulfilling work experiences. This trend will have a major impact on the work environment of the future.

The impact of the cocooning trend will be dramatic. Other substantial shifts in worker attitudes Compounding to the turbulence will be some. Things just won't be the same anymore. We'll explore these fascinating transformations in the next chapter.

7

Trend Shifting Worker Attitudes

Worker attitudes will continue to shift from those of traditional loyal servants to those of strong-willed independents. These changes will cause conflict between those traditionalist employees, old style managers, and "new" employees. Workers will place loyalty to their own careers ahead of attachment to any single employer. They'll be more interested in collaborating to get things done than in taking orders from any bosses.

The attitudes of workers at all levels are undergoing dramatic change. Their attitudes toward work are changing. Their attitudes toward their employers are changing. Their attitudes toward management are changing. Their attitudes about their careers are changing. These shifts have been stimulated by several factors. Part of the change flows from generational attitudes—and the differences between generations could fill a book or two by themselves.

Generational Differences

Let's first explore some generationally-inspired attitudes to understand the shifts. The values of each generation are definable and different from other generations. By necessity, since there are so many differences between people, these observations must be generalizations.

The "Parent Generation," those born prior to 1946, are more traditional. Their beliefs are that bosses have their place and workers have their place. They don't mix a lot. Workers do what the bosses tell them. If their direction is wrong, well, they're the bosses. They must know what they're doing; it's not our place to question or challenge them. They'll go along with whatever has been established.

The Baby Boomer generation sees the role of workers more as team players. Bosses are still bosses, but they should take workers' ideas into consideration. Management doesn't always have all the answers. Young people have a lot to offer, but they have to earn the right to participate by sincere dedication. Boomers will conform to expectations, but seek to make some changes when it's their time to be in charge.

Members of the Baby Busters, the 13th Generation, or Generation X, are more independent. They feel they should have more of a say in how things are done in their work environment, especially when it concerns their jobs. They want more control over their lives—including how much time they spend at work, how they work, and where they work. Busters are ready, willing, and eager to make any changes they can.

Employer Attitudes Toward Workers

In days gone by, employers felt a serious responsibility to employees. A number of companies even built company towns with nice homes and even shops for the workers. They hired people to work for them for a long time. Job tenure of 20, 30, 40 years or more was commonplace.

Employers and employees felt they each owed something to the other. Employers were benevolent figures. If the management style was tough, the description used was "benevolent dictator." The sense of responsibility felt, and exercised by company owners was comparable to a parent's care of children.

Layoffs were avoided. Employers took care of their own, and everyone pulled together. Employees were as loyal to their owners as the companies were to them. There was a partnership sort of feeling between management and labor.

In those cases where the workers didn't feel they were being treated quite the way they wanted, they organized into unions. But, even with the presence of unions, there was still a loyalty—almost a family feeling—between workers and employers.

During this period, most companies were run by the people who founded them—or at least by their direct descendants. The family name and values held a great deal of importance.

In recent years, there has been a dramatic change in employer attitudes and behavior toward workers. In the past, company ownership was more paternal, and policies affecting workers were more benevolent. Many of those family-owned companies went public through sales of stock or were purchased by conglomerates. In many cases, owners and managers who had known each other—and their workers—since childhood, were replaced by hired professional managers from out of town.

Company loyalty to workers was supplanted by obligations to stockholders. The stock price, dividend level, and bottom line replaced the care and protection of workers. The long-term commitment evaporated in the face of tightening costs. Relationships yielded to impersonal business decisions, often made from some remote headquarters location.

In the early 1980s we saw the beginning of this trend of impersonal decision making, but it wasn't widespread enough to cause alarm. We heard cries from around the country about employer requirements to notify workers if plants were to be closed; employers resisted the interference with their right to make decisions. Concern was not high, since the sense of loyalty and caring for workers still seemed to be there.

In the late 1980s and early 1990s, employers were again faced with the need to cut expenses. And personnel expenses were a logical first target. Layoffs, early retirements, and other techniques were used to reduce payroll. Suddenly, a lot of long term employees found themselves out on the street. While some employers were very sensitive, a number of companies demonstrated a callous disregard for their loyal employees during this process of shedding redundant personnel. Thousands of employees experienced a cold, formal severing of the relationship they believed was a sort of almost familial contract. A bond had been broken, and many felt betrayed.

Mergers and acquisitions, ownership changes, and plant closings have distanced senior management from workers. An understandable alienation has evolved from this distancing. The general feeling among a lot of employees today is that it's futile to show loyalty to the company when that loyalty won't be returned. It's become an issue of trust.

Now, a disclaimer. Not all employers were as heartless as those I have just described. Some were actually very caring and the separations were effected with a lot of emotion. Some employers even helped their displaced employees secure new positions with other companies. However, so many employees experienced an absence of loyalty from employers that a serious chasm of distrust grew between workers and company management.

Even if people did not sense this attitude at all in their layoff, they probably felt it indirectly by hearing stories from friends, neighbors, and relatives about the negative way these others had been treated. Regardless, the present tendency is to distrust employers. Employees no longer feel inspired to be loyal.

By understanding this shift in perceived company loyalty to employees, it's easy to appreciate why employee attitudes toward their employers are changing. The "cradle-to-grave" concept of lifetime employment is history. And we probably won't see this attachment again.

Now, and in the future, employers will have to *earn* employee loyalty. Long-term allegience won't be automatic anymore. A great deal of the strength and stability of the workforce will be dependent on the relationships that managers and supervisors build with their workers.

Management Attitudes and Behavior

The evolution of management attitudes toward labor will continue. Workers will welcome the shifts toward collaboration and openness. Changing management behaviors will encourage a continuation of the current cooperativeness of labor unions.

Most of today's managers, particularly senior managers, were raised in the "old" school of management philosophy. They learned autocratic approaches that worked fine years ago when employees expected a boss to tell them what to do. Traditional styles of directive management are less effective today, and are often seen as counterproductive.

While more modern managers, generally younger people, are more people-sensitive and supportive, they are under the influence and/or control of the traditionals. Inherent conflicts develop between the more firm, autocratic managers and the more loose, democratic managers. This comparison is not to say either is right or wrong, but to appreciate the impact of their conflict on other employees.

A large proportion of employees don't want to be told what to do, step-by-step. These workers don't want a supervisor looking over their shoulders all day. They want to be included in the decision-making process to determine desired results, shown what to do, given the support they need, then given the freedom and trust to get the job done.

What employees want and what supervisors deliver has been in conflict for about two decades. The rift has become more apparent in the last 5-10 years, exacerbated by the tension surrounding the post-recession tightening.

Managers and supervisors are changing. Well, some of them are changing. Others are resisting change. Still others are trying to change while listening to senior management complain about costs.

Workers are changing, too. Employees struggle between waiting to be told what to do, working along with the supervisor, and taking the initiative. It's difficult for them, because they often hear different messages from management and can't tell what management wants. The temptation is to tell management to get its act together. Meanwhile, the customers are still demanding the goods and services the company is expected to produce.

As both groups wrestle with what they want—and what they want from each other, there will be tension. . . and anxiety. The process of people trying to redefine their roles and relationships will continue to cause turbulence in

most employment environments at least through the end of the decade
. . . and probably far beyond.

Some Current Attitudes

Current employee attitudes offer us insight into what we can expect over the next 15 years. Let's explore a few of these perspectives.

Independence comes up very strongly. Tomorrow's workers will place a high value on self-direction. Higher levels of accountability go along with that self-responsibility. With this desire for autonomy, we can predict some culture-shaking changes in relationships within the corporate setting.

The self-management motive will move a higher proportion of workers from traditional roles into new positions. Many will become contractors, home-based businessespeople, or work at home or in satellite work centers for their employers. Work hours will become more flexible for many positions as the emphasis shifts to achievement, not just activity.

Learning is an important value for the worker of the future. Expect strong attitudes about employers providing education and training resources, growth opportunities, and time off to pursue further knowledge and understanding.

Dress will become more casual in the workplace. We've already begun to see some trend in that direction in the mid-1990s. It will become stronger as we move into the future.

The casual dress is symptomatic of more casual attitudes around relationships. As corporate hierarchies continue to flatten, we'll see more collaboration in the workplace. This posture will be difficult for some managers who fear they won't be needed anymore. This fear is blocking true employee empowerment in many companies.

Realignment of positions and responsibilities will continue to cause turbulence in the workplace. Workers will test new arrangements, only to have them changed again by management, themselves, or circumstances. Questions like "What's going on around here?" will be prevalent.

Prevailing attitudes about employee-employer relationships and responsibilities to the company will shift. More workers, and their employers, will regard work relationship as talent for hire. . . and often for a deliberately short time.

A relatively new concept called "career resilience" will become accepted in the work environment. Essentially, career resilience involves employers offering professional growth opportunities to workers. The workers join the company to learn skills and make a contribution to the company's objectives.

Once the worker is no longer growing or can no longer make a viable contribution, he/she then

Once the worker is no longer growing or can no longer make a viable contribution, he/she then moves on to another opportunity to upgrade knowledge and skills and make another contribution. The employment relationship is understood by all parties, so there are no "hard feelings" when the relationship is ended by either party.

Human resource researchers have suggested that a truly viable career period with a given employer is 8-10 years. Around that period, both employer and employee are beginning to realize diminishing returns. In the faster-moving work and learning environments of the future, we can expect this time frame to be tightened to 4-6 years. The average time spent on any one job will be less than five years. Experience, learning, and impact will happen much faster in the future than it did in the past.

Shifting worker attitudes will be difficult for many employers to accept. The process of change will involve a considerable amount of negotiation, of give and take. This metamorphosis will be complicated by the dynamic nature of the workforce, with workers joining and leaving continually. New hires will bring their experiences and perspectives from previous employment(s), "infecting" the change process like a virus.

Hang on! It will be a wild ride!

Demands for higher levels of productivity and the resultant higher levels of stress further complicate the picture and contribute to the turbulence. The effects of this stress will speed up the change process, and could turn everything upside-down.

8

Trend High Productivity, High Stress

High productivity has been achieved, but at great expense. Stress levels are so high among workers, their performance, thinking, and loyalty are at risk. Thousands of employees are receptive to any opportunity to move to a more relaxed employment environment. They're looking for the greener grass on the other side of the fence—they're sure there's something better out there.

A different kind of feeling has begun to permeate the workforce. We might even use the descriptive word to characterize the workforce in many companies. The word? "Resentment."

This new attitude can be found among workers in all industries and, interestingly, at all levels of employer organizations. The trend that brought this feeling to the surface will persist, so we'll continue to observe its side effects.

Here's what happened.

As employers felt the squeeze of the 1989-91 recession, they felt compelled to reduce the size of their workforce. On the surface, that was a reasonable strategy, seeing that personnel expense obligations are usually the largest single category of operating costs.

Employees were dealt some serious emotional stress as they saw their co-workers get laid off, "rif-ed," or enticed with hard-to-decline early retirement packages. In many cases, workers "lost" people who had become valued partners and good friends over many years.

Sometimes the force reduction was gradual, sometimes a large number of employees were given their pink slips all at once. This tightening was painful, with dramatic struggles to quickly stabilize the remaining workforce.

Remaining employees watched how their colleagues were treated during the downsizing; their memories are strong. Emotions run high, especially among the remaining employees who must now shoulder a heavier load. . . and bear the stress of increasing demands on every member of the team.

Combined with the grieving for this loss was the fear that any of the workers remaining employed could be the next to go. These tight-sizing changes were received differently at each company, depending on how the employer and managers handled the situation. Some were given reassurances, but the next wave of layoffs often nullified any hopes—or trust—still held by employees.

The next phase in the tight-sizing was potentially more damaging than the removal of co-workers. It was the realization that the volume of work would not change. Before the remaining workers had a chance to be thankful they still had jobs, their workloads had increased significantly! Those left behind had to pick up the load that had been carried by their departed fellow workers.

Now, let's be realistic. Picking up the slack wasn't that difficult in many companies. A great many employees really hadn't been working at full capacity. They were able to assume the additional load without too much of a problem. Except, the increase in the volume and intensity of work did foster some major changes in how people perceived their jobs and how they got tasks done.

A number of workers, accustomed to less-than-a-full workload felt pushed. Cries of "unfair!" were drowned out by the comfort of still being employed. This acceptance of their plight did not mean these employees were happy, or even content.

Against this backdrop, the workload continued to increase. Contributing factors were more layoffs or resignations, work reassignments, and additional work due to increased business. In many companies, workers selected to remain employed were expected to show their appreciation by doing whatever was necessary to get the work done.

Employees were rarely given extra support to enable them to carry the heavier load. Most did not even have the benefit of training in time management, setting priorities, or project/process management. With corporate reshuffling, a lot of employees found themselves trying to tackle tasks in new positions they had not been prepared for. Many found themselves derailed from their career path, a shift which contributed to their discomfort, alienation, and anxiety.

As if these circumstances weren't bad enough, these overwhelmed employees found that the customary 37.5 to 40-hour work weeks just wouldn't get the job done. But someone had to do it. With fierce dedication, people worked late and spent some week-end time on company business—in the office, at home, or somewhere else. These demands generated family irritation that the worker wasn't enjoying life with them.

Through all this turmoil, we can all be proud that productivity was up for American business. Of course productivity was up! More work was being completed by fewer people. Our noteworthy performance scores belied the undercurrent of dissatisfaction.

Workers were under stress. In almost every company in almost every industry. Tempers flared. People quit. Work didn't quite get done the way it was supposed to. The core problem was attitude.

In some instances, the intensifying stress led—directly or indirectly—to violence. The news media covered some of the workplace violence, but certainly not all of it. Not expecting violence and certainly not trained in how to handle it, managers and supervisors absorbed even more stress worrying about it.

Management personnel were hard-pressed to get their jobs done. A dangerously high proportion had not been sufficiently trained to perform in their roles of increased responsibility. In fact, a surprising number had never received supervisory training at all! Without adequate training, many supervisors were simply not capable of doing the jobs assigned to them.

Conditions in many organizations could well be described as chaotic. And, in spite of the fact that some consultants and management theorists say chaos is productive, the people experiencing this situation didn't see much good in their predicament.

Unfortunately, these beleaguered employees felt trapped. With the impression that there were no other jobs out there, they had to stay where they were. This feeling of helplessness contributed to the stress and disengagement.

Interestingly, some of those workers who complained about the stress while working 37-40 hours a week will leave their employers and go into business for themselves. They will be excited about having control over their incomes, but they'll be working 50-60 hours a week or more to make their businesses successful. The stress will be different, however, because they'll be in charge of their time and their lives.

Yes, workers at all levels have been carrying a heavier load. But their employers, while aware that people have been working much harder for longer hours, have been slow to add more employees. This moderation has been influenced by the enjoyment of high productivity and uncertainty in Washington.

Employers lament the taxation they have to bear. While this message is certainly not a new song, the confusion surrounding healthcare and other employment tax liabilities has dampened employer movement to put more people on the payroll.

Gradually, employers will employ more workers, probably hiring more carefully. Qualified, competent, experienced people will be hard to find; the task will be difficult. A number of the people who will be hired will shift from higher productivity/higher stress environments. . . hoping for something better.

Wise employers will be sensitive to these emotional issues when hiring and assimilating new hires. Through this process, work can be redistributed to balance the burden. This process will be an opportunity to shift the culture to one of less pressure and a more comfortable, collaborative flow.

As you can imagine, the re-assignment of work will be a delicate process. Those overstressed workers have become attached to their responsibilities and will be reluctant to release them . . . and perhaps take on other duties with which they are not familiar or comfortable. Some workers will leave. Some will resist. Some will be relieved, see the big picture, and want to help.

There will be a period of unsettledness during the readjustment. In most companies, the expansion of the workforce will not be easy. As business increases, the workload will also increase. The resultant instability, uncertainty, and expanding demand will combine to create dynamic tension and confusion: continual turbulence.

Imagine walking through your company's facilities and feeling a vibration in the floor under your feet. A constant vibration that won't stop. . . and sometimes changes in intensity. How would you feel about that sensation? Combine that feeling with a sense of the noise and light levels changing in a random pattern. Would you feel uncomfortable, nervous, on edge?

Workers will feel the same sort of off-balance sensations, the same sort of sense of being out of control. Some workers have been feeling this uneasiness for a long time. They've gotten used to it. They're numb.

It's not a pretty picture, but it's reality in many more work environments than you'd believe. In my work as a consultant, I see it frequently—not just with my own clients, but in places I visit in my travels. Fellow consultants share similar perceptions of what's happening in their clients' workplaces. You've probably seen it, too.

As a consequence of the push for productivity and lean operation, many disoriented employees simply "attend" work. They're present physically, but psychologically they may be absent. It's all become a blur.

Other employees are angry, very angry. Some have resorted to violence. Most will resist attempts to engage them in employee involvement programs, total quality initiatives, or even company social events like picnics.

Employees are feeling the full range of emotions and responses to stress. This condition is apparent in business, government, and not-for-profit organizations today. Psychological problems, physical health maladies, emotional outbursts— they're all there. For many employees, work is a love-hate experience, but necessary to satisfy personal needs in life. A common attitude is that employees love their paycheck, but hate their job.

Enlightened employers will deliberately raise their sensitivity to the high stress and its effects as they make any kinds of changes over the next few years. This period is a time for an extra dose of humanity, of caring.

Special attention should be devoted to working mothers. Despite talk about men sharing responsibilities of parenting and household management, most of the burden still falls on the women. The transition to more equal sharing will take a while. In the meantime, career women who are also mothers have stress at both work *and* home. Expect these workers to carry home problems to work. . . and work problems home. Help them with the balance with a little extra sensitivity. Obviously, this same message applies in the case of single-parent fathers and fathers who are heavily involved in family management.

Some employers will provide special training for their managers to help them work through the adjustments. We'll see employers hire psychologists, sociologists, and other consultants to assist them. The focus of attention will be that employees are the company's greatest asset.

In other situations, employers will conduct business as usual, with no increased sensitivity. Expect to see greater impacts of the turbulence in those places. Some of those employers, proud of their survival thus far, will not make it through the next shift of cultural emphasis from high productivity/high stress to a more balanced work environment.

A great deal of worker stress is caused by the attitudes and behavior of their superiors. And no wonder! Corporate leaders are confused themselves. Why? A long history of conflicting style emphasis, combined with a lack of management training, has left managers ill-prepared to lead. The leader of the future will facilitate more than manage.

9

Trend
Changing
Leadership
Styles

Employees are confused by the inconsistency of styles used by their managers. They have difficulty discerning congruence of purpose and values, let alone how to do things. Leadership and management styles are changing; a more collaborative, facilitative style is emerging. New approaches will be required to manage in continually changing work environments.

"O.K. I'm a boss. I'm proud to have been promoted, but what do I do now?"

That strange sort of statement has been on the minds of countless supervisors over the years. All too often, we promote people without giving them a clear understanding of their new roles. . . let alone guidance in how to make the transition from the old position to the new. I call this process "Promotion by Anointment." Here's how it works. . .

A vacancy occurs, and we look around for the most likely candidate. We pick an employee who's been doing a good job on his/her present assignment. Our assumption is that he/she will do well in a higher position. Makes sense, doesn't it?

So we promote our best salesperson to sales manager. This poor victim has no idea how to be a manager. In one quick action, we've lost our best salesperson and are stuck with an inadequate sales manager. It happens all the time.

The chosen one is brought into the Big Office for The Promotion Ceremony. The senior manager waves a magic wand and sprinkles some magic dust. Poof! We now have a fine new supervisor, manager, director, vice president. . .

With no training, mentoring, or any guidance whatsoever, this potential leader is doomed to failure. We need to give our fledgling leader some strong, effective leadership training, a mentor, and frequent, realistic coaching.

Let's start with leadership style. Actually, we don't have to. Our new appointee has been watching other managers for years. The style is apparent. . . or is it? If this illustration represents most companies, each of those managers practices a different style of management. Our new supervisor is confused, but that's all right. So is everyone else in the organization.

Does that sound harsh? To suggest that so many people in organizations are confused by the incongruity of leadership styles. . . or lack of them? It's a malaise of the corporate world today. And the government world. And the not-for-profit world. And that confusion is causing serious disillusionment that demotivates employees.

Managers who do have an opportunity for training learn everything from autocratic methods to open styles where employees are encouraged to take initiative for their own work. Most courses and seminars deal with a variety of styles, without concentrating enough on technique. The technique programs are usually offered by employers, but without assuring that everyone learns and supports the same style(s). Result: more confusion.

As long as leadership style incongruity continues, organizations of all kinds and all sizes will experience turbulence. To succeed in the future, leaders will learn about human and organizational behavior. . . then make some serious decisions about what style(s) will work best for their "community." All leaders will then be expected to adopt the selected style to build consistency throughout the organization. Achieving this congruence will not be easy.

To appreciate the emerging leadership styles, it's helpful to gain a little historical perspective. Management—as art or science—has gone through some significant changes during the past few decades.

The autocratic leadership style underlies much of the management practices today. It's a strong, directive, hierarchical style that has been practiced successfully for years. Bosses enjoyed telling workers what to do, and workers accepted comfortably their role of doing what they were told.

Then some enlightened management theorists suggested that managers ought to listen more to what their people had to say. Managers should still have the power to make the final decision, the theorists advised, but gathering input enriches the decision-making process and supports worker commitment to the final solution. This participative management style is still actively used today to stimulate involvement.

This participative style worked so well, some managers and theorists wanted to go further. The next phase in the development of leadership styles was team management. Now managers were expected to get workers together in teams to make some of their own decisions. Self-directed work teams came into vogue as the organizational hierarchy continued to flatten.

A lot of employees are not comfortable working in teams. Others are very happy to work with others, but become unsure of the validity and value of their own contributions. A large proportion of workers want to be recognized for their individual accomplishments, not melded into a faceless team.

Given the trends we have explored in this book, I envision another leadership style emerging. I have named this new style "facilitative leadership." Essentially, facilitators (managers) focus on each individual performer working for them. Their objective is to work one-on-one with those individuals, helping strengthen their effectiveness in the work environment.

The idea is to help each individual employee reach his/her own potential. Goals are set high, then managers and employees work closely together to reach those goals. . . and stretch even further. Team issues are not even considered, because the emphasis is on each individual. Teams are not even *explicitly* formed by management.

Teams, when not dictated by work assignment, will form themselves. With a conducive organizational culture, people will apply their uniqueness to building and maintaining an effective operating environment. This collaboration, these partnerships, will come from the employees themselves, rather than from a directive leadership effort. This more serious approach is exactly what's needed in organizations today.

Facilitative leadership techniques include mentoring, coaching, stimulating, and supporting. It's a sort of vertical collaboration in which the leader and individual performer actually help each other perform better at what they are expected to do.

In this design, there are no feelings of being threatened by someone getting more training, supervising more people, or being told what to do. The focus is on improving performance and achieving established objectives.

Facilitative leadership will fit nicely into the flow of what other trends will bring us during the next 5-15 years. Emphasis will be on the individual, consistent with the resilient career concept discussed earlier. But emphasis will also be on each employee really concentrating on what he/she is supposed to be doing to help the overall organization achieve its goals.

The individual attention aspect will also be well-suited for the management of employees working from their homes, from satellite work sites, and from "virtual offices." This shift will be essential: supervisors will no longer be able to observe what all employees are doing all the time.

"Distance Management" will be the new design. Many of today's managers and supervisors will have difficulty adjusting to this new style and, understandably, will resist its implementation. More turbulence! People will not work the same way they have in the past, so the management approaches of the past won't work.

Leadership in the future—the near future—will be based much more on trust than it is today. Employees will do their own work, based on the clearly-stated expectations of others. These "others" will be their customers: their bosses, the company as a whole, their department and/or other departments, and outside customers will be customers. Those in supervisory positions will also consider their subordinates as "customers"—consumers of their leadership and management guidance and support services. Ratings will be based, in part, on how well satisfied their customers are.

This internal concept of customer service will cause some turbulence, at least at first. Even though customer service has been taught and preached strongly for the past decade or more, service levels are far below acceptable levels. Consumers have been screaming more recently, but not enough to be heard in most cases.

Now we're going to give credence, birth to a new emphasis on employees having status similar to independent contractors with high levels of accountability. To get their jobs done, these accountable individual performers will insist on high quality responsive performance from their suppliers—fellow employees.

People at the same level in the organization will become more demanding of each other—a whole new kind of work relationship. Expect endorsement of this concept to be mixed. We'll see a lot of champions, as well as a goodly number of detractors. This process will not be an easy transition.

The leader and follower might be in the same building, perhaps even in close proximity. But, in the creative freedom of the workplace of the future, they could be far apart physically. The employee may work from home or from a satellite work center in the suburbs or in a remote community. The employee could spend most of his/her time on the road and in client facilities. The possibilities are infinite.

Establishing Expectations

Employees and their leaders will determine performance expectations during semi-annual or quarterly planning and role definition conferences, No, not annual sit-downs; these sessions will be more frequent because things will be happening so rapidly.

During these planning sessions, both leader and follower will articulate their expectations—of each other and of fellow employees, other departments, and outside entities. Part of the leader's role will be to engineer and support collaboration between his/her followers and those with whom they must coordinate.

The focus of discussion will be the results the employee is expected to produce. . . and what support the employee will need from the supervisor in order to accomplish their agreed-upon objectives. They'll talk about communications issues, logistics, and scheduling. The supervisor will want to see the employee on some sort of regular basis—weekly, monthly, or quarterly in most cases

The level of understanding, agreement, and communication between employee and supervisor must be considerably higher. This stronger connection will revolve around the periodic planning meetings. These sessions will be much more than mere interviews; they will be serious interactions, with both participants actively involved.

The connection won't stop with the planning sessions. The supervisor will engage in a close monitoring process that will be mostly coaching in nature. Conversations will explore achievements, difficulties, performance processes, and professional growth. Gradually, the supervisor will become more of a coach than a boss. The two employees will come closer together from a hierarchical perspective.

Coaching will be a vital component of the leader's role. Unfortunately, most managers have never been taught how to coach their people. Few of them have been coached during their career, so a new field of professional coaching will emerge.

The beginnings of this new field have already been seen. Coach University was formed in 1993 to teach people how to be coaches of others. A new technology was created, enabling highly effective coaching to be done through periodic telephone conversations. Based in Salt Lake City, the educational organization offers a 36-module training process. Obtain further information by calling Coach University at (800) 48-COACH [(800) 482-6224].

The founder of Coach University, Thomas J. Leonard, also developed a method he calls "virtual coaching." This innovative approach establishes a communications relationship using fax or e-mail technology. When coach and client communicate this way, both participants must put their thoughts in writing. More thought is involved and the focus shifts from maintaining a close interpersonal relationship to solving problems, removing obstacles, and helping ordinary people become extraordinary.

Relationships between supervisors and their subordinates may well revolve around fax and e-mail messages to a great extent. This change, again, will challenge leaders at all levels to think, relate, and communicate differently than they have in the past.

The technology already exists to support this type of work relationship. In fact, quite a few companies already have a significant number of their employees working without physical proximity to their managers—or each other. An increasing number of workers are using e-mail to communicate and get their work done. The technological capacity of a laptop or notebook computer has altered the way we work forever. And we've only just begun!

The proportion of these new designs compared to traditional arrangements is still very small when compared to the total employee population. Therefore, most supervisors have not yet had to manage people who aren't right there where they can be watched. The shift will be a challenge for them, for their superiors, and for the training professionals who will be charged with teaching people how to work this new way.

Expect a lot of turbulence as we move into and through the transformation to new work styles and the required new leadership styles. The transition will be difficult, time consuming, and potentially threatening to a lot of things we now take for granted in the operation of work organizations.

The difficulty with leadership shifts will be exacerbated by concurrent shifts in where and how we work. Since style and venue go hand-in-hand, the next chapter will shed some more light on what's happening.

10

Trend

Changing Work Environments

The familiar worksite of the past is rapidly becoming as extinct as the dinosaur. Locations and designs of work environments are changing, causing much discomfort for those who stubbornly want things to remain the way they've always been. As a counterbalance, some employers are making worksites more employee-friendly. This effort may be a case of too little, too late.

Most work environments have changed significantly over the past few decades. Government regulation has had a significant impact on health and safety, and unions have also had their influence over working conditions.

Most employees still go to central congregate locations to fulfill their employment obligations. This pattern has prevailed for most of the 20th century. And it will continue to hold true for the largest proportion of workers for at least several decades, since many occupations require people to work together in production or service.

People working on the same project or task were in close physical proximity. Supervisors were right there with them, communicating one-on-one in a directive manner. Each employee had his/her own workstation as assigned by management.

Most larger companies and government agencies were housed in multi-story buildings in downtown areas. Cities grew up around these central areas, attracting service, manufacturing, and professional companies that interacted with major manufacturers or government agencies.

As cities became congested, property became almost prohibitively expensive. Large employers found it increasingly difficult to expand near their existing facilities. As employers sought less expensive alternatives for growth, new plants and offices were built—in suburban, exurban, or rural locations.

With alternative work sites, a move to more open spaces was inevitable. Many workers moved to the suburbs, attracting downtown merchants to open branches nearby. Merchants discovered they were earning much more money from their stores in the suburbs, and sooner or later, closed their downtown stores. Downtowns began to die; coming downtown to work wasn't so exciting anymore.

During the latter part of this transition, worker values were changing, too. Workers objected to long and expensive commutes, crime, high costs for parking, air pollution, and old buildings that were no longer efficient. Applicants began to select their next jobs based on job site location. It was time for change. Workers were dissatisfied and employers were unhappy about high operating costs.

The transformation from high stress downtown employment sites to lower stress non-urban work locations began in the last decade of the 20th century. The first decade of the 21st century will see even more dramatic changes as this trend continues.

Suburban Locations

Employers of many types relocated to the suburbs. They found they could do business with the same, or even greater, productivity and cost-effectiveness. Workspaces were healthier, more spacious, and more efficiently designed than those in older, downtown buildings.

Movement to the suburbs will continue, but those areas, too, are becoming congested in many metropolitan areas. The advantages once held by suburban locations have diminished as a result of over-building.

Exurban Locations

The movement beyond the suburbs began tentatively in the early 1990s, then picked up momentum. This trend will continue, particularly with the advantages afforded by communications technology.

This trend will have some interesting implications for metropolitan development and traffic patterns. Since suburbia was opened as a life style after World War II and more strongly after the Korean War, the majority of workers have commuted to downtown job locations in our major urban areas.

The outward movement of employers will create a new phenomenon for workers. For the first time, we'll see more commuting traffic leaving the suburbs and going farther out instead of into the central city.

Satellite Work Sites

Companies located in the central cities have begun to establish satellite work sites in suburban locations closer to where their employees live. Some satellite locations are owned and operated by one employer; others are shared by several companies.

These remote sites are most attractive for housing workers who use computers, telephones and similar devices in connection with their work. It is also effective for people doing independent tasks where they need a quiet place to get their work done.

Some employers have arranged for employees to work most of a one or two-week period at the remote site, then travel downtown one day each week in order to coordinate and communicate face-to-face with people working there. . . or at other remote sites. We'll see less need for those downtown meetings as technology, including video communication, and people's comfort with it, make more open communication possible on a regular basis.

Satellite locations will make it more possible for working parents to be with their children at school activities. Working schedules will become more flexible as it becomes more convenient for people to work part of a day, take care of personal business, then later return to work. Working close to home will be a sought-after benefit.

The employer gains, just as the employee gains, by remote job siting. Less expensive real estate is needed, usually outside the more high-priced downtown areas, decreasing the company's cost of doing business. Productivity improves because of the increased efficiency and lower stress.

Work at Home

There has been a significant movement toward working at home—as employees and entrepreneurs. The shift was already underway when it was given a boost by widespread layoffs of white collar workers in the early 1990s. During this period, many former employees became owners of start-up businesses, operated economically and conveniently from their homes.

Employers discovered that some workers could do very well performing their duties from their home environment—at least during part of the week. A new term was coined for this type of worker: "telecommuter." As we moved into the mid-1990s, this trend did not gain much momentum. In fact, employers authorized more positions as home-work-eligible than there were willing employees to fill them.

With the advent of computers, modems, fax machines, telephone features like voicemail and teleconference bridges, and electronic mail, working at home is very similar to working in a satellite center. There isn't the same physical connection with co-workers, but such direct communication will be substituted with videophone or picturephone technology. Physical proximity and contact will be less important in the years ahead.

Work Virtually Anywhere

Technology that is already available and being used by thousands of workers has set us free from the necessity of working at a specific location. With a portable computer, all you need is a telephone line and you're connected with the world. With cellular and satellite technologies, even hard-wired telephone lines aren't needed to communicate from *anywhere* in the world.

Using computers, pagers, and cellular telephones, some workers have become so independent, self-sufficient, and productive, they don't even need to come into the office. Employers make some workspace available to these travelers, but that space consists only of a computer docking station, a telephone, and maybe a locker to leave some personal belongings in storage.

These workspaces are used by a number of people as they pass through the office, enabling the company to get much more productivity from much less space.

Employee Friendliness

Employees understandably make judgments about how their employer cares about them by looking at their workspace. If the work area is clean, bright, healthy, cheerful, employees feel valued and encouraged. If working conditions are less than what might be reasonably expected, the employees feel less worthy and their performance shows it.

In the recent past, employers of all kinds have demonstrated strong efforts to improve working conditions. Some employers have done a fine job of creating—and maintaining—high quality places for their people to work. . . and rest.

In many retail and service establishments, there is still a visible difference between the appearance of customer or guest areas, as compared to the areas set aside "behind the scenes" for employees. This disparity has negative consequences for the companies and is often reflected in the attitudes of their employees.

Many employers have deliberately improved lighting and the cheerfulness of surroundings. They've decorated break rooms and working areas, as well as the executive offices and the areas that customers may visit. Ergonomics have been taken into account in furniture and workstation design. Lockers are now provided in many establishments so employees can secure their belongings. Special convenience features have been added, such as anytime banking machines in places with enough employees to make installation cost-effective.

The place people work is important, and so is their relationship with co-workers. Those work relationships are changing, largely because of external factors, causing considerable unrest and turbulence. Imagine—instead of the master teaching the young apprentice, we're going to have young people who know more about new technology than master craftsmen.

11

Trend
Reverse
Apprenticeships

Traditional approaches to learning a profession or trade won't work anymore. The old role identifications and social hierarchy will be practically turned upside down. Conflicting velocities of career development threaten corporate stability. With the emphasis on computers, older workers will be taught and mentored by a diverse group of younger people.

For generations, more experienced workers have passed knowledge and skills to newer workers. In a number of occupations and industries, this process has been formalized as apprenticeship programs.

Those workers who were most experienced and proficient were described as "master craftsmen." Behind them, with less experience and expertise were "journeymen." The relative neophytes were called "apprentices." This well-respected hierarchy of seniority was most prevalent in the trades.

The system worked well for many years. Young people starting their careers appreciated the careful teaching they received from journeymen. Master craftsmen received well-deserved deferential treatment from the journeymen and most certainly, from the newer apprentices.

The same process was applied outside the trades—to sales and management workers. The terminology was dropped in such cases, and the ranking wasn't as obvious. Descriptions like "coaching" and "mentoring" were used to describe what was happening.

Respect for our elders reinforced the notion of older workers passing knowledge and skills down to younger people. Everything worked smoothly for years, as long as work continued to be done the same way.

Work Processes Change Status

With the advent of automation, the skills of the master craftsman didn't apply as strongly or directly. The process of passing techniques down from senior to junior members began to lose its luster. This relatively gradual change was difficult for a lot of trades workers to accept. It was discomforting to realize that the playing field was leveled.

Whenever this degree of change takes place, relationships change. Advantages are lost. . . and gained. A competition for relative "position" emerges. Turbulence sets in—unless and until new relationships are established and accepted.

The disturbance of the accepted social hierarchy on the shop floor created a discomfort among workers. This uneasiness contributed to the general feeling of disassociation that comes with change. Older workers who grew up in an era when respect for elders was paramount were unsure how to act as their patriarchal role eroded. Their juniors were just as confused.

Then came computerization. Experienced tradespeople had adapted pretty well to mechanical automation, but the advent of computers was frightening, intimidating. Computer Numerically Controlled (CNC) machines moved into the shop. Older workers were faced with a choice: learn or leave. It was a difficult time. Master craftsmen and journeymen alike had to learn the same new techniques. The line between their levels became blurred, then practically disappeared. And apprentices could do almost everything they could using the new machinery — sometimes better!

Advanced computerization went even further. Now older workers were bewildered by new technological applications that were almost second nature for the younger people raised on television, video arcades, and computer games. During the late 1990s, the Nintendo Generation will have much greater proficiency with the new technologies than the workers who have been employed for decades (doing just fine, thank you, without computers).

Imagine the turbulence that arises from these circumstances! The age-based social system of deference and leadership now has little basis. Young people feel they deserve at least the same pay earned by their older counterparts—long-time employees whose pay has risen over the years to relatively high levels.

The Velocity Issue

Older workers—let's generalize with a range of over 40—have a different level of energy, wisdom, maturity, and stability than younger workers. The older folks are focused on getting the job done for their employer. Many, particularly in the older ranges, are rather dedicated to maintaining the status quo. They've worked hard and don't want to rock the proverbial boat.

Younger workers approach their careers from a different perspective. They do want to shake things up. "Let's experiment with new ways to do things," they cry. "Look at what's going on out there!" they exclaim with a competitive motive to stay on the leading edge.

And they are much more aware of what is happening in their industry, in the country, and in the world. Raised by the electronic baby-sitter, they are at ease watching television and picking-up the latest from the "tube." Video and computer based training are effective means of instructing this group.

These young people (ages 20 to 40-45) watch Cable News Network (CNN) and read USA Today. They've become accustomed to making big decisions with just a little bit of information. They live "on the edge"—looking for the next new experience or opportunity. These relatively energetic young people move at a faster pace through life.

They are full of enthusiasm and energy, certainly in contrast to the older generations. And, while the older folks appreciate the ebullience of youth, they don't easily recall the high awareness, the self-focus, and the intense concentration on doing something significant at one company and then moving directly to another.

The generation of employees currently in the 10-30 age range will be much more technologically competent. They will move at a much faster pace. They won't be satisfied with waiting for something to happen; they'll make things happen!

Let me share a personal experience from my life to illustrate my point. When I graduated from college, I was recruited by a Fortune 500 company as an executive trainee. Supposedly, I was on a fast track to higher management. A year or so into my employment, after some experience in various assignments where I had proven myself, I was offered a career growth position as assistant manager of wage and salary administration at the corporate office.

My superiors and counselors seemed pleased with the offer they extended to me. I asked about opportunities for advancement. The "motivational" response was that my next move would be to become the manager of the department. And when would that be? When the current manager retired. He was only 55! I left the company soon after that to join a retailer who offered me a fast-track challenge.

Corporate managers will find themselves surrounded by young people who want to move through life at a much faster speed than their predecessors. They're willing to apprentice for a while, but not for long. They'll learn quickly and will resist being held back in any sort of structured program.

Some of the brilliant young people will want to re-shape older workers. They'll want to teach them computers, creativity, and innovation in a sort of reverse apprenticeship. The interaction between these two groups and the results could be quite interesting and productive.

Tomorrow's corporate human resources picture will behave much like a large river. Some water will flow slowly, but the main channel will, at least at times, flow very fast—encountering rapids, making lots of progress, and taking lots of risks.

Young workers, and many older workers, want more control over the flow of their careers. These forward-looking employees want to design and manage their own life's work, not merely progress at the whim of corporate management. Learn about that trend in the next chapter.

12

Trend
Self-Control
Over Career
Destiny

*Workers want more control over their work and careers. Employers, who have traditionally held much of that control, will relinquish part of their influence, but it will be a struggle. Self-directed employees will be able to select from a number of alternatives to manage their own careers. People may choose to work for several employers **at the same time** to build their own security and strength.*

In the United States and many other countries, there is a clear trend toward people gaining more control over their destinies. Our generations have shifted back and forth between orientations toward themselves and toward others. Various age groups have been described as the "me" generation or the "we" generation.

The orientation of today's workforce is largely self-centered. The "me" folks, the "we" folks, and the unaffiliated all have a strong interest in managing their own lives. Today, people want to take control so that others are not running their lives for them. People want to make their own decisions about what they do, where they do it, for whom, and when.

There are clear indications that we will see even more movement toward self-management in the next 5-15 years. Part of this shift was stimulated by the recession of the early 1990s. Workers who suddenly found themselves out of a job had to fend for themselves. Record numbers of laid-off workers, including many former mid-level managers, started their own companies. They took charge of their destinies.

Another shift toward self-management flows from the natural attitudes of the younger generations. This is particularly evident among late Baby Boomers and the Baby Busters. They express a drive to be more independent, to have more control over their lives. They are reluctant to conform; they want to march to the beat of their own drums.

Some shifts are enabled by corporate belt tightening and management philosophies. With fewer people to get work done, each person must take more initiative. With fewer people in management, self-leadership becomes more important. Employee empowerment efforts are encouraging more self-direction, management, responsibility, control, and accountability.

Let's begin by reviewing some of the background that contributes to the worker attitudes we'll see in the years ahead. Historically, most people worked in traditional employer/employee relationships. It's been the standard (and still is), although we see increasing departures from tradition.

For years employers have hired people to perform particular kinds of work for specified compensation. The employer set the rules, including work hours, procedures, hierarchy, growth and advancement, and relationships with other workers. People did what they were told to do when they were told to do it. . . or they were given creative career redirection opportunities.

Employee-employer relationships were long-term. When a young person was hired by a company, the assumption was that the individual would be employed there for many years. Lengthy job tenure was the norm, often reaching 30 or 40 years. Workers did not see that they had a lot of choices or control over their situation. With limited mobility or awareness of outside opportunities, employees contented themselves with whatever job they had. A large proportion of people worked very close to where they grew up—in many cases for the same company one or both of their parents worked for.

In earlier generations, workers would trust their career development to their employer. Most workers would remain with one company for many years, gradually moving up the organizational ladder in their chosen field. Few workers took the initiative to look for jobs in other companies—in their town or anywhere else.

The majority of workers stayed in their same fields. People were identified by their occupation; there was no motivation to switch. Occasionally, high-performing employees would have opportunities to change fields as their careers unfolded with their chosen employer. Or, displacement from one position forced the worker to accept another position in a related—or much different—field. Transitions were sometimes difficult, but the multi-field growth was gradually seen to be positive.

Some employees would find themselves in circumstances that forced them to change employers in order to continue their career growth. These moves were usually made somewhat reluctantly, often within the same industry or line of work.

Loyalty to one's employer, occupation, field was highly valued.

Today's employees have been "burned" by employers who are not as loyal to their workers as they were in the past. Plant closings, reductions in force, mergers, and other major changes have hurt employees badly. Even if a particular company has not engaged in these actions itself, employers in general have a reputation for not being trustworthy because of their strategic shifts over the past few years.

Wary employees have learned they must fend for themselves in the development of their careers. They must assume control over their own destiny. Loyalty to any one employer becomes secondary to personal investment in one's career.

Today's philosophy is simple: if employers won't be loyal to their employees, then why should their employees be loyal to them?

Six different employment scenarios will be seen during the next 5-15 years. In each case, workers will become more assertive, more independent. This shift will stretch the management capacity of employers; some simply won't be able to work with non-traditional approaches. They risk becoming dinosaurs as workers insist on different relationships with the people that give them paychecks for their services.

The first scenario is the traditional relationship of the worker being on the payroll of an employer. The company managers direct everything the employee does. The worker is a part of the organization, performing at the pleasure of the employer. The employer is clearly in control.

The second scenario is a variation on the first. In this case, the employees have considerably more control over their lives than in the first case. This difference may be seen as employees leading themselves as self-directed work teams. Employee Stock Ownership Plans (ESOPs) may fit here as an expansion of this category, depending on how much influence employees really have over day-to-day and long-range operation of their company.

As employees assert themselves even more, we'll see traditional employment situations modified by employees who want more control over their working lives. They'll negotiate—usually on an individual basis—for working hours that suit their personal schedules, how jobs will be done, how much vacation time and non-paid time-off they'll have, and even how their performance will be measured.

Does this sound like the tail wagging the dog? It will seem that way as employees gradually perceive themselves more as individual performers working under an internal, bi-lateral, full-employment contract for their employers. They'll still be full-time employees, but with much more control over their relationship with their employer.

These people will be known as "empowered employees," and the concept will extend far beyond workers who believe they have some minimal responsibilities and involvement with making the employer successful. Working within the framework and guidelines established by the employer, these diligent workers will have a wide range of employment opportunities. They'll be assertive, pushing to be sure they have the resources and support to accomplish what the employer wants to have done.

A third scenario will have workers contracting their services to the employer. They'll be independent contractors serving at least one employer, probably several employers over the course of a year. Some will describe them as "temporary" workers and, as compared with permanent employees, they will be.

These contractors will be hired to work on specific projects or to participate in short-term assignments. A lot of the relationships will be temporary. However, there will also be long-term engagements with varying hours or less-than-traditional full-time hours. If an employer only needs someone for one day a week, say, or four hours a day to perform a particular task, contract employees may be the answer.

Professional positions will be filled this way in many companies. Since the early 1980s, some of my colleagues have earned their living as contract professionals for several employers. One of them is a contract personnel manager for several firms. He schedules his time, in collaboration with his client companies, to be at each company when, and as, needed each week.

With over two decades of experience in his field, this man charges each client a fee that, on an hourly basis, would be higher than the companies might pay (hourly) for a full-timer—if such a person were needed. But the companies only pay for the hours actually worked. Everybody wins.

Another colleague performs the same way as a corporate controller—serving several employers each week. None can afford him on a full-time basis, but they all benefit from the time he works with them.

The next 5-15 years will see a trend toward more of this individual contracting. People will come up with some creative ways of establishing themselves as private contractors—talent for hire. They'll enjoy a new sense of freedom and control over their lives, and will influence others to follow in their footsteps.

I anticipate that we'll see people of all ages become contractors, but a high proportion of them will be workers who have gained at least 10 years' of experience. Many will be older workers. The early retirement programs of the late 1980s and early 1990s created second career opportunities for people in their fifties and sixties. We'll also see more military careerists entering the private sector workforce as a consequence of downsizing in defense industries.

This segment of our workforce will have gained sufficient experience to have proven capabilities. They'll have the maturity to manage themselves, and the financial strength to step out on their own. It will be scary, at first, to be without a steady paycheck from a single employer, but that fear will dissipate as the contracting business is built.

Some independent contractors will work 40 or more hours a week. Others—older workers and those desiring time for other endeavors—will work fewer hours. They'll enjoy the freedom of managing their own time. Some will even create businesses to serve and support other independent contractors.

A fourth employment scenario will involve an amalgamation of independent contractors. There will be at least two variations on this theme. The motivation to come together will be a combination of the strength-in-numbers feeling and practical needs to share expertise and mutual support.

One approach will be contractors working together, formally and informally, as a cooperative. These may or may not be comprised of people working in the same field. Cooperative members may share in billing services, benefit programs, and even establish a group office. . . hiring clerical support (or including members who can provide needed support services.)

Another approach will be the formation of more businesses to contract with independent workers and arrange assignments for them. Instead of being "head-hunters," they'll be job/assignment hunters working on behalf of the independent contractors. Their strongest market will be the contractors who don't want to get involved in their own marketing and sale of their time. These contractors will seek others to handle that aspect of their work, so they can concentrate on their assignments.

We're also seeing arrangements where professionals contract to a brokering firm. In this case, the driving force is the broker, not the contractor. Professionals remain independent contractors, but get most of their work through the broker. The broker handles the marketing and the billing, paying the contractor for work performed.

We'll see specialization in this field. Already emerging are firms that lease specific kinds of workers to a number of employers. An example is the firm that arranges long-term, and short-term, assignments for professional engineers. Each of the engineers works as an independent contractor to one or more clients at a time, with details of the business relationship handled by the firm.

I predict that these entrepreneurial ventures will be an outgrowth of the temporary service industry, already enjoying an increase in business in the mid 1990s. The difference will be in the firm's orientation to its clients. Temporary agencies view the employer as their customer. The emerging contracting agency will view the contractors as the customer.

A fifth scenario has also begun on a relatively small scale, but will grow in the years ahead: employee leasing. In this case, the leasing company hires most, if not all, of the workforce of a company, then leases the workforce back to the employer. When providing this service to a number of employers, the leasing company is often able to provide stronger benefits to each employee involved with the program. The workers are actually regular employees of the leasing company.

The employee leasing idea is being utilized by employers opening new facilities. They simply contract with the leasing firm to recruit a workforce for them. This system works well because the leasing company, specializing in human resource functions, does all the recruiting, screening, hiring, benefits orientation, and personnel administration tasks. Some leasing companies even provide training for its employees.

One benefit of the leasing arrangement is that employers don't have to get involved in termination proceedings. If the employer doesn't like the way a particular employee is performing, or just doesn't want that person around for any reason, the leasing company simply gives the employee a new work assignment.

There is a nice advantage for the employee: the same option is available. If you don't like your assignment, your supervisor, or the company you're serving, you can usually be reassigned to another position or another company.

These changing employment relationships generate some difficulties—some challenges—for workers. employers, and leasing companies. A number of issues must be clarified. Those concerns range from supervisory authorities to legal liabilities, to tax obligations. These matters will gradually be resolved, although wrestling with the government will present some challenges. These new designs don't mesh with current laws, so there will be turbulence in these arenas until matters are resolved.

As an afterthought to this discussion, let's not forget the rise in home-based businesses and outsourcing. These trends are congruent with changing employment relationships.

During the early 1990s, we saw a new trend of outsourcing—principally in the industrial sector. This shifting of responsibility took two forms.

One outsourcing approach was the contracting with one or more outside suppliers for specific services that had previously been provided in-house. Motivations included improved efficiencies, cost savings, and a desire by employers to concentrate all their resources on their core business.

The other approach involved selling entire support departments to outside vendors or to the employees who worked in those departments. These transfers were handled as leveraged buyouts and some were set up as Employee Stock Ownership Plan companies.

The emerging companies often continued to operate in the same space, following the leased department concept used in many retail operations. These new ventures were also free to seek work from other customers, which was often a motivation to make the change in ownership.

These trends in worker/employer relationships all have their impacts—individually and collectively. But there's more. In addition to the trends there are several influencing factors that compound the predicaments faced by so many employers.

Section 2
Influencing
Factors

13

Influencing Factor
Changing Workforce Demographics

Significant shifts in the composition of our workforce will have a major impact on business during the coming years. The changes in numbers and types of workers will be unsettling because the kinds of people working will be different than what we have seen in the past. The movement has already begun, and will continue at an ever-increasing rate.

1. The workforce is growing at a slower rate.

There is already a shortage of qualified workers in many areas of business, and that shortage will become more acute. A drop in the birth rate in the late 1960s is having a measurable effect today.

The growing need for workers has been satisfied for years by the Baby Boom generation. Over 76 million people were born into this generation, from 1946 to 1964. As the economy expanded, these Boomers were there to fill the jobs. And, when the economy tightened up, the Boomers felt the impact.

As the Baby Boom generation drew to a close, the birth rate began to drop dramatically. The generation that followed the Boomers, known as the Baby Bust or 13th Generation (also called "Generation X"), includes only 68.5 million people.

Employers are now feeling the shortage of applicants. There just aren't as many people in their teens and twenties. Employers quite naturally became accustomed to the flow of new workers. The cornucopia was overflowing. The more-than-adequate flow lulled employers into complacency.

Suddenly, it seems, there are fewer responses to newspaper ads for applicants. "Help Wanted" signs stay up longer, and are less effective. Many employers still think there are lots of people waiting outside their doors, eager for any job they have to offer. Not so! Now, as employers open their doors, they are astonished to discover that no one's there!

2. The workforce is getting older.

The average age of the American worker is climbing. By 2000, the Census Bureau estimates, the average age will be 38.6 years. In the late 1980s, the average worker was 35.2 years old.

As Baby Boomers continue to age, with improved nutrition and healthcare, we can expect to see the average age go even higher. It stands to reason: people are living longer and fewer people are being born. The average age of the population increases.

So what? The aging of the workforce means more older workers, relatively speaking, than younger workers. The maturity levels will be higher. They'll have a better sense of what they want. . . and may be outspoken about it. They may change jobs less often in later years, particularly if benefits are not portable. However, without having to worry about keeping the kids in school, these older employees may be even more apt to leave—even travel across the country for a new job in a different geographical region.

Older, less mobile workers may need some accommodations. I'm already seeing benches by elevators in office buildings, ramps instead of stairs for short rises, railings, and other senior-sensitive considerations. As people get older, they may be reluctant to accept new technologies. They may not want to work full days. We may see older workers developing attitudes of independence similar to those we'll see in very young employees. Anticipate some interesting values conflicts...inter-generational and intra-generational.

The retirement age will continue to creep upward. By 2010, it will be commonplace for people to work into their 70s and even their 80s. The first wave of the Baby Boomers will be 64 in 2010, but won't have the resources to completely retire.

Some employers will be tempted to dangle the carrot of early retirement, repeating the strategy of the late 1980s. It will be costly to employ a lot of older workers in their peak earning years. But early retirement programs will only serve to reduce the number of people employed by the company. The retiring employees won't be easy to replace, short-term or long-term, with younger people. There won't be enough younger people to go around!

Result: employers will negotiate new relationships with older workers. They'll want to keep them on-board to tap their expertise and experience. There will still be a lot of work to be done. But these older workers may work fewer hours or perform less strenuous work. These shifts and limitations will create some interesting work assignment and design challenges for employers.

3. More women will enter the workforce. . . and they'll move into more influential positions.

There are several reasons more women are entering the workforce. One is the need for additional resources in families, producing two-income households. It costs more to maintain desired standards of living, and college tuition is getting more expensive all the time.

Women are also entering the workforce to pursue careers, instead of just working at a job. It's a new orientation to the reason for working. For many women, it's much more than merely money. The number of single (female) parents is also on the rise, deliberately in many cases. Many of these women are driven, for one reason or another, to be definitively self-supporting. And an increasing number of women want to remain single, following a different path than their mothers and grandmothers.

Multiple-income families wrestle with complicated schedules, shifting societal relationships and interactions. Mothers and fathers are already playing some different roles. This shift will accelerate, partially fueled by burnout of one partner or another. The work/responsibility load will become heavier.

Employers will receive more requests for creative working arrangements so one parent or another can be home with the kids. Counterbalancing earlier generations' acceptance of latchkey kids, future generations will seek more close relationships with their children.

Women in influential positions will change their style of leadership. Women have been socialized during their growing-up years to nurture. The importance of relationships and communication have been taught since early childhood. Girls learn different styles of conflict resolution than boys do. Their socialization influences women to lead others differently than men do.

The conflicting styles of male and female socialization, combined with generational conflicts, contribute to the sense of unsettledness in many organizations. These differences must be resolved carefully in order to create a new kind of "teamness." This will take a while, so expect a certain tension. It's part of the turbulence of this era.

4. Diversity will become a greater part of the fabric of life.

Popular attention to workforce diversity has focused attention on the vast range of distinctions between people. We began our concern with diversity with racial issues. Then we expanded our attention to include cultural differences.

As people from varying backgrounds came together, we described the United States and its institutions as a "melting pot." Diverse cultures were seen as melting together into some sort of conformist homogeneity.

The chemistry wasn't working. Many people, proud of their unique ancestry, wanted to maintain their own identities. The "melting pot" became the "mixing bowl." The soup became a tossed salad. We concentrated on accepting differences between people. Live and let live.

Initially, the spotlight of workforce diversity was simply focused on how we are dissimilar—skin color, religion, ethnicity. This focus has broadened, and—more importantly—the filter has changed. The trend has shifted.

Our attention to diversity has been to protect certain groups of citizens/workers—mostly driven by regulatory concerns. Gradually we have gone beyond the requirements of law to devote more attention to the uniqueness of individuals. The protected group concerns of race, age, gender, national origin are now only a small portion of the picture of who a person really is.

With this emerging approach, the focus is on *valuing* the differences between people. We now seek diversity in our hiring to deliberately avoid a homogeneous workforce. The emphasis is on building a workforce comprised of many different kinds of people—people who can each contribute something special to the whole.

We're in the midst of a shift from diversities separating people to a cultural environment where diversities will actually bring people together. The trend is more to value differences as part of the reason we're together, instead of a reason to stay apart. We have learned that we can all be together, even though we're different. It's a new appreciation, a consciousness that flows from a variety of societal influences.

Each succeeding generation has placed greater value on individual differences. This bias is particularly evident among the late Boomers and the early Busters. The 13th Generation, now moving into the workforce, is much more attentive to individuals than to group norms.

An increased sense of mobility also supports the mixing of individuals. People of all sorts of backgrounds are moving into the same neighborhoods. They see each other as individual neighbors, rather than encroaching groups, because of the multiple diversities. More than ever before, we can have a wide range of ethnic group members living on one street.

5. Concept of Diversity Expanding

Our working definition of diversity has expanded considerably over the past few years. We now consider. . . even value. . . all kinds of diversity. The differences between us give us different perspectives. As those perspectives are brought together in a positive way, the results are powerful!

Here's a list of some of the many categories of diversity seen in today's workplace. There are many more diversities than most people think!

accent—regional, different language
age (and how you feel about your age)
automobile—kind(s) owned/leased
behavioral style
birth order
birth place—hospital or other environment
brain—right or left
career orientation
children—number, ages. . . relationships
clothes—type worn, preferred
college—size, private or state school, major
commute to work—method, distance, time
computer literacy—depth, IBM/Apple
conflict—method of handling
credit—amount, attitudes, usage
debt—amount, type, comfort
education, level attained
education, public or private
entertainment preferences
experience in foreign countries
facial hair
food preferences
gender
golfer or not
hair—color, length, baldness, own or
        manufactured
handedness—right or left or ambidextrous
health
height
home—rent, own. . . where

languages spoken
leadership—abilities, interests, experience
length of employment
literacy
lottery—player, winner
lunch—bring or buy
management experience
marital status
music preferences
national origin
number of jobs held in career
parents—attitudes, living or not
pets—ownership, type
politics
race
rank in the work organization
reading—preferences for magazines, books
religious background, orientation
residence—length of time in community
sexual preferences
siblings—relationships
smoking—yes/no, experience, attitudes
sports—degree of interest in
television—amount and types of shows
          watched
travel—interest, experience
vacations—number, length, activities
volunteer involvement
wealth—current and readiness for retirement
weight—and attitude about it
wellness, physical fitness

where raised—urban, suburban, rural

And the list goes on and on. Each individual's mix of background and preferences affects that person's attitudes and behaviors.

The workforce is becoming increasingly diverse in many ways. Managers in the future will relate more with individuals than with groups or teams. To accomplish this constructive connection, managers will learn and apply much more knowledge and skills in interpersonal relations.

14

Influencing Factor
Educational Deficiencies

While, on the average, today's employees may be better educated than previous generations, they won't be prepared for the jobs that will be available. Many of today's graduates are insufficiently equipped, or barely equipped, to perform the jobs of today and tomorrow.

Our society has placed more emphasis on formal education in the last 20 years. We have seen some worthwhile improvements in the quality of public education, but there are still serious concerns. Experimentation with a wide range of educational programs has taken its toll. Many students experienced confusing inconsistencies in teaching approaches, and were often victims of the testing of new teaching methods.

The emphasis on learning computer skills has left many students unable to spell (spell checkers on computers take care of that) or calculate (computers do that, too). Employers complain that recent graduates lack creative thinking skills.

While many schools are returning to the "basics," a lot of current and new entrants to our workforce lack the fundamentals. The National Council on Excellence in Education reports that 13% of 17-year-olds can't read at an eighth grade level. Deficiencies like this will create dangerous problems for us in the future, when a higher proportion of jobs will require literacy skills.

Competency tests, administered under state guidelines, are reinforcing standards around the country. It's interesting to watch reactions to the testing program and its results. A feeling of pride and almost smugness is evident when a school system produces high scores.

Unfortunately, most school systems are not earning high scores in the standardized competency tests. When students get low scores, the parents seem to complain about the tests instead of asking why the students haven't learned what they need to know. And the teachers argue that they shouldn't have to teach to satisfy a particular test.

The fact remains that these competency tests have been carefully designed. . . and they're revealing that we're not yet producing the product we need from our educational system. This insufficiency will have a serious impact on workplace performance if it is not corrected. We already have a generation of graduates who are ill-prepared for the world of work.

There is a bright glimmer of hope on the educational horizon. As of this writing, 50 school districts across the country "guarantee" their graduates. The schools guarantee to the employers that the graduates they produce will all meet agreed-upon standards of competency. If they do not, in the employer's opinion, the student will receive whatever remedial education might be necessary at no expense to the employer or the student. We'll see more of this trend, but only after some thrashing about and tough negotiating within the political arenas of the school systems.

While people will be generally better educated than previous generations, they won't be prepared for the jobs that will be available. Entry standards for many jobs have risen over the past few years. That trend will continue, based on the use of technology and other expectations of evolving jobs. Some of the reasons for raising entry standards are legitimate. Others are based on societal shifts such as a college education having a value similar to what a high school education used to have.

Employers will need to hire workers. The dilemma will be whether to try to hire people who can perform all the tasks associated with the job, or accept the condition of needing to provide training and education to most new hires.

As a whole, the people standing in those lines seeking jobs will be less qualified for the jobs to be done, forcing some employers to hire "warm bodies" and invest considerable sums in training marginal applicants to perform at levels that will satisfy their customers.

15

Influencing Factor

Obsolete Workers

Many people currently in the labor pool, particularly older workers, are obsolete. "Obsolete:" well-trained and experienced to perform jobs that no longer exist. Some of these older workers are still employed, because their employers have decided to take care of them.

In some cases employers haven't yet been able to upgrade to more qualified workers. Many obsolete workers were "dumped" on the unemployment lines during the restructuring and upgrading process that followed the 1989-91 recession.

This dumping isn't over yet. As energetic young people with computer literacy skills are recruited, employers will remove workers who have been with them 5-20 years. These workers, who are loyal, dedicated, and hard-working, will be confused, angry, and disillusioned. They will find other opportunities, though, because their talent will be in demand by other employers. Some retraining may be necessary to qualify for those opportunities.

In many occupations, work is performed much differently than it was just a few years ago. And over the next 5-15 years, there will be even more substantial changes in the way work is done. This shift means that we have a lot of fine workers who need to be re-trained—many for jobs that are not at all similar to what they did for most of their careers.

The key to future work success is adaptability. Few workers—in any field or at any level—will do things "the way they've always been done." What worked 20 years ago probably won't work today. In fact, what worked *two* years ago probably won't work today!

Learning will be the most important skill. Success won't depend so much on what a worker can do now as it will on how easily the worker can learn and perform the new skill. This capacity to learn will be vitally important—for entry level workers as well as for those who have a great deal of experience.

Workers who have gone to schools—secondary or post high school—where they've learned how to learn will be in the best position in the future. Young people entering the workforce would be well-advised to learn how to learn.

Employers will be faced with serious, time-consuming, and expensive challenges to upgrade the workforce. This upgrading will range from teaching basic literacy skills to older workers who didn't need more than an eighth grade schooling when they started their careers, to building competence and confidence in high level computer skills.

More emphasis will be placed on interpersonal relations and self-management training. What have been described as "soft skills" will grow in importance. Expect growing recognition of the importance of human-to-human communication and collaboration, with a supportive movement to strengthen skills in these areas.

Consultants and trainers will be in demand to help satisfy the growing need for training and development in the organizational setting.

Section 3
Forecasts

16

Forecast

Unprecedented Churning in the Labor Marketplace

As demand continues to increase in a growth economy, employers will start hiring again. They will be much more cautious and selective than in the recent past. Only those applicants who meet tough qualification standards will be hired. Then they will be expected to perform at a high level to maintain healthy productivity.

As this scenario unfolds, the most qualified workers will be harvested from the unemployment rolls. Those that remain unemployed will need re-training to compete for the jobs that will come available in the next phase of economic growth.

Employers will still need to hire qualified, high performing people. If they can't find them readily at the unemployment office, they'll start recruiting people away from other companies, government agencies, or not-for-profit organizations.

This movement to recruit people already employed will begin concurrently with the end of "corporate cocooning." Many employees targeted by recruiters will be quite receptive to invitations to make career moves.

As the trends discussed in this book interact with each other, workers will begin moving from their current jobs—or unemployment—into new jobs. Some of those jobs don't even exist today; they will be created by a growing economy that emphasizes technology, information, and service.

Economic growth will stimulate increasing demands for qualified employees, and the most qualified employees will be quite willing to leave uncomfortable situations for new and exciting opportunities. They will assume that the "grass is greener" on the other side of the fence, and they will jump eagerly.

As the economy heats up and more opportunity-seeking workers change employers, the job-changing will become a socially accepted, perhaps socially *expected*, thing to do. Workers will be actively and openly looking for change, and employers will need them. Employers will need them because business is getting better. . . and because they'll need to replace the employees they're losing.

Considering all we have considered thus far in *Turbulence!,* you can see how I can predict . . *.an unprecedented churning in the labor marketplace.* I see this churning beginning mid-decade, around 1995, and continuing at least until the end of the decade before it calms down.

In my work as a professional speaker, delivering keynote speeches and general session presentations to trade association conventions and corporate management groups, I have explained what I see in the trends. I have warned the top executives in my audiences about this coming churning.

Invariably, after I speak, people from my audiences will talk with me one-on-one. They have been telling me since late 1993 that they have already seen signs of this churning. In late 1994, I heard much more about this subject from these business leaders.

Essentially, employers will face employment conditions that will be unlike anything they have

ever experienced. . . or even expected. And few
employers are anywhere near ready for what's
coming. Most companies, government agencies, and
not-for-profits are dangerously vulnerable.

Many employers, still believing that there is
an abundant supply of qualified applicants just
waiting to work for them, will imitate the ostrich.
They'll stick their heads in the sand of "look how
good it is now," refusing to accept that we live in
turbulent times. They simply won't recognize that
their position may not be as secure as they think it
is.

This denial makes about as much sense as
learning that a hurricane is headed your way, but
insisting that your property won't be hit. Things like
this always happen to "the other guy."

The Unstoppable Downward Spiral

"So, what can happen from all this? So we
change a few players on the team. The game goes
on." Does it?

Let me paint a scenario for you, a scenario
that could—and will—happen to a lot of companies.
Follow along with me and see if this story makes
sense to you.

The Fictitious Corporation (TFC) has been in
business for three generations. The company has a
decent share of its market, with a many satisfied

long-term customers. Those valued customers are served by employees who have been around for a while; they have good first-name relationships.

Competitors persist in their efforts to nibble away at Fictitious' market share. They continue to call on TFC's customers—offering to be of service, building relationships for possible future business.

TFC experienced some tightening up during the first half of the 1990s. Some senior employees were lured into early retirement with lucrative severance packages. Newer employees were laid-off. One department was shut down as its work was outsourced. A smaller division of the company was eliminated when the TFC board of directors decided to drop a product line.

With productivity up and profits rolling in nicely, the TFC stockholders are happy. The board has praised the company's senior executives for holding the line and "running a tight ship." Everyone seems to be working hard. There's a lot to do, so many people work long hours to get the job done.

The economy seems to be heating up, even though the news media keeps reporting negative indicators. Something's going on out there—TFC's customers are doing well and placing more orders. In fact, the entire industry is in a growth mode.

Like its competitors, TFC has hired more people to handle the increased workload. These new people don't know their jobs very well yet, but the more experienced workers are there to teach them, mentor them, and provide needed leadership.

The human resource department has been directed to begin building a list of qualified, pre-tested applicants who can be called when business warrants more hiring. Management has strategically used a just-in-time approach in employment—do the recruiting ahead of time, so the people are ready to be hired when they're called.

The recruiters are having mixed results. Some job applicants are eager to leave their current jobs for new employment. Others, including some specific individuals the recruiters have targeted, seem hesitant to commit to joining TFC. Something about the way the layoffs were handled a couple of years ago has gotten around.

A production line foreman turns in his resignation. He's been recruited by a competitor who is setting up a new mini-plant to produce a new product. TFC's foreman will become the manager of the facility. His co-workers are happy for him— "great opportunity!" "Wish I could have. . . "

A senior account manager is recruited by one of TFC's suppliers. A newer sales representative leaves to join a customer's company. In a shuffle of assignments, other TFC employees assume their customer contact responsibilities. The affected customers are uneasy; their relationships with TFC were with the people who left. They don't know these new people.

Meanwhile, TFC's competitors have learned about the salespeople leaving and have stepped up their efforts to earn new business. Some of the competitors are pretty confident, because they've concentrated on building a stable, committed workforce of loyal professionals. TFC's customers sense that confidence as they learn more about these other vendors..

The production foreman who left discovers he needs some more people to help him. Naturally, he invites some workers he trusts to join him. Productivity and morale drop in his old department at TFC. The same change is observed in an adjoining department when its foreman leaves to become a shift leader in the new plant.

Employees of four other TFC departments leave to accept similar positions outside the industry. Remaining employees watch their colleagues leave and wonder if they should be staying. They see more ads in the help wanted section of the newspaper, and some get phone calls from recruiters. Two design engineers are recruited by a start-up company in a related industry. They'll have equity in the new venture.

New employees have been hired, but they need time and attention. Some of these new workers need a lot of help. The human resource people have found recruiting of quality applicants increasingly difficult; they've settled for applicants who didn't meet all the company's standards. Productivity drops as experienced employees, who had been hard-pressed to get everything done before, now have to devote time to teaching new people.

Sue, in production, gets upset because George from TFC's maintenance department can't find the parts to fix her machine. George is frustrated. He doesn't know where to look. Norma knew "where that stuff was," but now Norma's working for a company out-of-state.

George's wife, Alice, who works for a different company, has been frustrated in her job, too. Alice's employer just doesn't give her the support she needs to get her job done. Alice has been asking for training, but her boss won't send her because he himself hasn't had any training for years. Why should Alice get it if he can't? She might learn more than he knows and take over his job.

Alice is considering a job offer from still another company two states away. George encourages her; he'll find something else in their new town. Alice accepts the job, and George becomes a "trailing spouse." TFC will have to do without his expertise and experience.

TFC's customers are complaining about quality problems, late shipments, and not knowing who to talk to in their efforts to get satisfaction. They're beginning to try out TFC's competitors to see how well the other suppliers can perform. TFC is losing business.

Beverly, the manager of accounts receivable, sees what is happening. The company's business is falling off during a period of business upturn in the industry. This situation doesn't look good. "Seeing the handwriting on the wall," Beverly accepts a position with an accounting firm in town.

One of TFC's major customers shifts orders for one product to a competitor. The loss of production volume means that TFC doesn't need all those people working in the departments that produced the product. Most of those affected are laid off. All but three are hired by other companies within a week. Two others enter another company's employer-paid training program to improve their literacy level while they learn how to work on a manufacturing team with a robot.

Word of the layoff spreads like wildfire. Other TFC employees begin to leave, fearful they may be the next ones to get layoff notices. Other employers target TFC employees as being receptive to reasonable offers.

With fewer experienced employees, TFC is having a more difficult time meeting customer expectations. More customers defect, cutting into TFC's cash flow. The vice president of human resources accepts an identical position with a new company moving into town. Recruiting becomes more difficult. The vice president of quality and her assistant join with quality specialists from two other companies to form a consulting firm. Finding no other way to monitor quality, TFC becomes the firm's third client.

The TFC controller decides not to take this pressure any more. He's tired of balancing receivables with the credit line and juggling payables in order to make payroll each week. He accepts an attractive internal management position with an investment banking firm.

TFC's competitors, who worked for years to improve their systems and involve their employees, are doing very well. Their efforts to build a highly competent workforce, emphasizing employee retention, have paid off. Business is great! Market share is growing nicely. Employees are happy and proudly recruit their friends to work with them.

TFC, proud of sticking with traditional management approaches, is in trouble. Senior management insists that the company stay with the proven systems and policies that worked for the president's grandfather. "If it was good enough for Frederick Fictitious, it's good enough for us today."

Unfortunately, Frederick Fictitious is dead. And so soon is the company he founded.

This scenario will be played out in a number of companies over the next ten years or so. The most vulnerable employers will experience this downward spiral beginning as early as 1995. Some will close their doors by 1997!

17

Forecast
The Future
Work
Environment

Work environments of the future will be dramatically different from those of the past. . . or the present. They'll have different purposes, designs, locations, and relationships to offer employees. The shifting need for different kinds of work environments—spaces, places—will affect how people relate to their work space and their co-workers in the future.

The majority of employees will continue to work at congregate job sites. Manufacturing production workers, most medical personnel, store-based retailers, and numerous others will see little, if any, change in their work arrangements. Others, particularly those involved in information gathering, sharing, and dispensing functions will experience considerable changes over the next 5-15 years.

An increasing proportion of workers will work in small remote work groups or alone at remote sites. More will work independently—on the road, at client sites, or at project locations. Even more will work at home—for other employers and/or in their own businesses.

Home-Based Work

Working at home will become increasingly popular, especially for working parents with responsibilities for child care or elder care. Futurist Marvin Cetron in his book, *American Renaissance*, predicts that about 22% of all employees will work from/at home by the turn of the century.

There are some interesting advantages that suggest that the number of people working from or at home will increase substantially in the next 5-15 years. The surroundings are familiar and comfortable. Wasted commuting time is eliminated, leaving more hours in the day for personal activities

. . .or more work. Home-based workers avoid the stress of commuting, and their automobiles will last a lot longer.

Workers will experience fewer interruptions working at home. For most, it will be easier to concentrate, so their productivity will soar. Home workers, appreciative of the flexibility in their work/personal lives, will be more loyal and will probably work a little longer than if they had to leave promptly at 5:00 to meet their carpool or take public transportation.

The movement toward working at home will stimulate attention to creating compatible work environments in homes. Some employers will fund remodeling projects to prepare space in employees' homes for their kind of work. More people will purchase homes with work space as one of their selection criteria. Astute real estate developers will build specially zoned residential communities specifically for those households that operate home-based businesses.

Communications between and among workers will be a major issue. The familiar concept that "it's lonely at the top" will gain a companion phrase: "it's lonely working alone." Even with the benefits of solitude, workers will want and need to communicate with others. In traditional employment, most familiar today, employees go to a congregate site. They communicate face-to-face every day; they're accustomed to continual interaction. Workers will seek creative opportunities for communication, probably extending beyond customary business hours.

Videophones will be used frequently to maintain the visual human contact that is so important to some people. Communications technology—already available and in limited use—will enable rapid real-time data transfer during meetings, simultaneously with human-to-human visual contact. This kind of open communication will practically eliminate the need for most face-to-face meetings.

This alternative to face-to-face get togethers can save time, but managers will need to pay special attention to building and maintaining human relationships. Frequent voice contact by telephone will be essential, and managers will visit team members in their home or remote site work environments. One of the major challenges during this turbulent period will be how managers will effectively oversee and support people working for them from remote locations.

Continuing education and professional growth will be a challenge for people working out of their homes. Educational and motivational television programming via satellite will link home-based entrepreneurs with ongoing learning and inspiration. An initiative leader in this emerging service area is The People's Network, based in Irving, Texas. For information about this service, call (800) 562-5877.

Characteristics of Come-Together Environments

The workspaces where people come together will go through gradual metamorphosis over the next 5-15 years. Work environments will become much more people-friendly, much more flexible, and much more "wired."

People-friendly features will include more windows and improved lighting. More attention will be given to noise control and the flow of healthy air. Ergonomic furniture will be complemented by cheerful colors and decorations that are more pleasing to the eye.

If they have enough employees to make it reasonably cost-efficient, employers will offer cafeterias with healthy meals (including carry-out service for employees with families to feed when they get home). Others will provide such services as hair care, shoe shining, anytime banking, and sundry store shopping to make common personal tasks more convenient for employees. This availability of shopping will expand the old company store concept into a whole new dimension.

Modular office designs will allow for changes in use of floor space whenever necessary. We'll see more common space, almost like condominium offices, where workers will share services and conference areas. The environment will be much more open than has been seen in the past.

Some workers will have moveable work stations. They'll move their workstations into proximity with others who are working on the same project as they are. When the project is done, they'll roll their work stations to attach to their next work team.

Congregate workspaces of the future will be designed for more sophisticated communication. Applied technologies will include fiber optics, cellular systems, and satellite utilization. This level of communication capability will be essential, since so many of the company's employees will work at places far from where other employees will be.

A substantial portion of the congregate worker's day will be spent communicating with and coordinating among other people. Each employee will be able to communicate with other employees, customers, or suppliers. . . wherever they may be on the face of the earth. Time zone differences will extend workdays world-wide, probably creating more jobs to facilitate rapid response from global inquiries.

Traditional Workspaces

In spite of the numerous changes that will take place in corporate/government work environments, we'll still have work places like retail stores, hotels, hospitals, and personal service facilities like dry cleaners and restaurants. There will be significant changes in these kinds of work sites.

Electronics and computerized interfaces will permeate all aspects of our working world. More retail stores will install interactive computer and communications technology that will report every sale and instantly order new merchandise for daily re-stocking. More of the same technology will be applied in restaurants, hotels, and personal service establishments.

Similar technological upgrades will be seen practically everywhere, placing some companies at risk. There will be a dangerous tendency to succumb to the glamour of the technology, letting good ol' customer service slip.

Expect application of technology in the workplace to be "dumbed-down," to make it simple to operate and understand. This adjustment will enable wider use by less literate employees, as well as speed up processes for those who don't want to take too much time learning to use complicated tools.

Factories will improve the working environment for the production workers who labor there. More automation will come, along with new jobs for people who can maintain the robotic and other sophisticated technology that will be installed. Brighter colors of paint will be seen, along with other appropriate site-specific improvements.

Human Turbulence

The dramatic changes coming in work place design will be unsettling for a lot of employees who have been very comfortable with things the way they've always been. Very few things will remain as they once were.

Some of the modifications will simply be change for change's sake, but most will be productive and, in fact, employee-driven. Employees will probably resist, to some degree, changes that are made unilaterally by management.

Employees who opt to work at home and/or at satellite worksites will find the adjustment a bit more difficult than they expect. Similar difficulties will be experienced by their colleagues who now need to work with them in very different ways.

The systems that had worked well for years won't "fit" the same way with a number of employees working at dispersed locations. Employers and employees will encounter some challenging upheaval as they go through the transition. Taining programs to ease the adaptations will come into vogue, as employers explore ways to facilitate the transitions.

18

Forecast
Changing Work Relationships

Psychologists at least as far back as Sigmund Freud have pointed out that work is one of the essential sources of self-esteem and meaning in life. For most workers, the employment experience has also given them contact with other people in ways that met their human needs for socialization.

Over the next decade or two, we will see a lot of changes in the way we work—individually and together. Work is being re-defined on an almost daily basis, causing a great deal of turbulence for those who find constant change difficult to handle.

Well, hang on! We've embarked on a journey that will see a lot of change before things settle down. . . if they ever do. As a result of the trends discussed earlier, we're in the midst of the most profound change in the world of work since Henry Ford introduced the assembly line.

In the past (and the present) most work relationships, those alliances between employer and employee, were characterized by relative stability, security, consistency and continuity. Not any more. The concept of stability vanished as computerization melded with corporate reorganization. Practically every company is looking at itself with a clean slate, starting over in response to a wide range of outside stimuli.

Most work relationships will still feature the age-old concepts of shared economic interests and shared responsibility. But how that will appear on the organizational chart will remain in a state of flux, of evolution. The work to be done is changing, as are the places we do it, who we do it for, how fast it has to be done, and who is best suited to do it.

Our emphasis used to be on full-time employees, supplemented by a few part-timers and an occasional temporary employee when someone was on vacation. Not any more. The proportion of full-time employees has dropped dramatically and will continue to drop in the years ahead. The percentage of contingent workers—part-time, contract, and self employed—is rising as a percentage of total employment.

The bulk of the work will be performed by part-timers (some long-term employees, but still part-time), contract employees, and temporaries. Companies will operate more with 7-day work weeks, with a fluctuating workforce that will be adjusted continually based on what work needs to be done. Individual employees will probably have shorter work weeks or work different hours than we typically see today.

Instead of one full-time job, many employees in the coming years will work at two or even three part-time jobs. Many will earn at least part of their income performing work at home, often with computers. This approach will suit some two-income families juggling responsibilities for children, housework, shopping, childcare, eldercare, and personal interests.

To achieve the flexibility that tomorrow's employees will desire, employers will cooperate in establishing job sharing, job splitting, varying work week schedules, and much more self-determination of actual working hours. There will be a shift to custom-tailored employment, causing employers to re-think the way work is divided and assigned.

This custom-tailoring will be fine for highly organized calendar-managing workers, but it will wreak havoc on close coordination, work planning, and payroll management. Yet employers will find it necessary to go along with what valued employees request—their need for good talent will force them into cooperation.

Employers will simply have to adjust. They'll respond to worker requests to adjust hours, job design, even fringe benefits. Multiple income households will have multiple benefit programs. Workers will want to divide benefit responsibility and funding among all employers involved so the household gets all the benefits desired.

This highly personalized "cafeteria" approach to benefits will work for the employers, too, saving them the cost of over-providing. Expect to see some creative benefit designs in the years ahead. Wellness programs will become even stronger with health club memberships a sure bet. We've already seen the beginning of benefits for non-traditional household partners such as gays and lesbians. As more people live together without getting married, we'll see an increase in the recognition of domestic partnerships.

The many varied work arrangements will require much higher levels of communication in the workplace. Fellow employees who don't work at the same time will communicate through electronic mail, by leaving messages on telephone and eventually, video voicemail systems, and by direct telephone calls even though at least one participant might not be actually working at the time of communication.

Workers in the future will be much more involved in setting their own job direction, managing their own performance. Their superiors will serve more as coaches, supporting workers in achieving the desired and agreed-upon results.

Fewer managers and supervisors will guide their employees with the methods that are popular today. Instead, we'll see more leaders practicing a facilitative style, inspiring and supporting the highest possible performance of each individual employee. The traditional relationship between boss and subordinate will be altered forever as the distance between leader and worker contracts.

Only very large organizations will have more than three levels of management. Computerization and employee self-management will eliminate the need for stacks of middle managers.

We'll move closer to this condition as the empowerment movement continues to grow. True empowerment will be a bit slow coming into its own. Two reasons: managers are afraid to let go—if they don't have and use power, what is their role? Are they really needed anymore? The other barrier is the employees themselves. They're afraid of assuming that power, and the accountability that goes along with it. After years of someone else telling them what to do, making their own decisions is scary. Human resource professionals have some serious work to do here, but it will be—*must be*—done.

Workers will gradually assume more and more responsibility for themselves and their work. To achieve their objectives, they'll learn the skills of partnering to better work with others. Teams will be formed as needed by the workers themselves, not management.

The results of reengineering and organizational restructuring will shake up more relationships. The old hierarchy, represented by the big Organizational Chart, is a relic of the past. Collaboration will be the successor as employees strive to work together.

Workers and managers together will make decisions about who will do what work. They will confer on how work should be done, even down to the design of production systems, customer service programs, and design projects. As teams, employees at all levels will seek ways to maximize the investment of human resources.

Training will be emphasized to a larger extent . . . at all levels and for all positions. Employees will voluntarily make themselves more valuable through cross-training. It is estimated that, between now and the year 2000, corporations will invest $150 billion (with a "b") in training and development for their employees. Workers will also invest a considerable amount of money in funding their own development—supplementing what they gain from their employers.

Front line workers will collaborate with management to determine when work should be outsourced, if contractors should be hired, or if temps should be brought in. Those front line workers will work hand-in-hand with management to maximize productivity from outsiders.

As more workers discover they really don't have to go to the office everyday, we'll see a surge in telecommuting. More employees will work at home, at least part of the week. This new who's-at-home-when pattern will cause turbulence in neighborhoods coast-to-coast. Men will be home during the day in some households, women in others. In some cases, both partners will be working at home, some of them working together, and some of   them   separately.

The impact of this shift will be dampened by the tendency for more women to work. Schools and other community organizations will have to make some major changes in scheduling PTA meetings and other functions. Participation in these activities will continue to wane as parents become more committed to different work patterns.

Tomorrow's workers will be much more mobile; they'll work from different locations—perhaps in the same day. Portable computers, combination pager/cellular telephones, and other tools will enable many workers to be "virtual"—able to function from anywhere. As we go to press, I already have a working "500" area code number that follows me wherever I go. This developing power will have a major impact on how employees work—alone and together.

The development of communications technologies will give even more power to smaller companies, putting them in an even better competitive position against much larger companies. Workers will be much more aware of competition as employers become more open about sharing corporate financial information. The partnerships that emerge between worker and employer will be powerful!

Service industries of all kinds will benefit greatly from virtual organizational concepts and expanded communications capability. By 2000, it is estimated that 88% of the workforce will be employed in service industries, so this growing operating strength will be increasingly important. Service industry companies will still employ a large number of lower level workers, but will increase their capacity by providing the training and tools that enable them to perform at a much higher level of efficiency and effectiveness.

As service companies expect their employees to work more with technologies, they will have to raise their standards of hiring and performance for all employees—including those at the lowest levels. Tasks that are now performed principally by physical labor will require greater skills and intellect as technological support changes the nature of the way work is done.

Women will play a much larger role in organizational leadership, which will threaten a lot of older (50+) male managers. These women will apply the nurturing skills they were socialized with to build strong, sensitive, caring, and cohesive teams and companies. This new leadership style will be a major shift—for a lot of people and a lot of companies.

Employment was largely a man's world for the first forty-some years of the century. In those days before automation, work was labor-intensive. Even well into the second half of the century, the type of manual labor required was more suitable for men than women.

As automation reduced physical requirements, more women began moving into the workforce. The entry process was slow, at first, since women were culturally seen as belonging in the home. Now with computers and other technology, women are able to compete very effectively with their male counterparts in many occupations. Their social skills often are much stronger than those of their male counterparts.

The increasing numbers of women in the workforce will want more than just money. Flexibility will be highly important to them. They will want time to raise their kids and do things for themselves. Employers, eager to benefit from their expertise and style, will offer women special considerations such as fitting their schedules around school days/hours and other family responsibilities.

Men will clamor for equal treatment. . . and get it. We'll see a rise in husband-wife teams working for the same company—sometimes in very different positions, often as a team working on a project together. This circumstance will come about as one spouse is recruited by an employer and brings the other along as a condition of making an inter-city or inter-state move. Employers will assume responsibility for finding a position for the trailing spouse—the easiest solution will be to hire both of them.

19

Forecast
The New Breed
"The
Adaptables"

Employees who prepare for one career and attempt to stay in one job type for their entire working lives will find significant competition from an emerging new breed of worker.

In the future—concentrating on the next 5-15 years, the most successful people will be "The Adaptables." These workers will be "light on their feet," ready to shift quickly in response to outside stimuli. They will easily adapt to changes in work requirements, job opportunities, and even major career shifts. Eager to accomplish their life goals quickly, they will live practically all aspects of their lives in fast-forward.

Adaptables will be self-sufficient. They'll prepare deliberately and carefully for the work lifestyle they've chosen. These workers will have a number of characteristics in common, yet each will be an individual. Let's explore some of the attributes of the Adaptables:

Education

Most Adaptables will be fairly well educated. By the turn of the century, they will have a minimum of two years of college. A large proportion of Adaptables will attend college classes—most to earn their (next) degree, some simply to acquire new knowledge or spend some time engaged in intellectual pursuits. According to recent statistics, those employees with higher education will earn the highest incomes in the years ahead. Education will have a higher value for them.

The most popular baccalaureate educational background, particularly after the turn of the century, will be a liberal arts curriculum. Students will seek courses of study that give them greater perspectives and understandings of "big pictures" without spending too much time on detail. Based on their early life media exposure, they'll want a CNN/USA TODAY style survey of a wide range of fields.

Some will develop a stronger interest in one subject or another and will take in-depth courses for greater insight and detail. Much of this specialization will be developed at the post-baccalaureate level. Worker/students will place emphasis on acquiring knowledge that will be useful, that can be applied in the work environment.

Capacity to Learn

With the world of work changing so rapidly, Adaptables will be confronted continually by new technologies. Their work requirements will shift with the introduction of new products, with changes in the marketplace, rearrangements of work teams, and other influences.

To easily respond to this myriad of new challenges and opportunities, the Adaptables will cultivate and hone their ability to learn quickly. They will read, study, listen to audiotapes or watch videos or compact disc images on their computer screens. Adaptables will continuously learn and grow professionally in a variety of ways, some of which haven't even been developed yet.

These knowledge-hungry workers will expect their employers to provide or at least fund a major part of their learning. Corporate recruiters will use professional development programs to entice top talent to join their companies. . . and hopefully to stay for a while. Employers that don't provide deliberate growth opportunities will find it much more difficult to attract the people they want or to keep those they have acquired.

Flexibility

These fast-trackers will enjoy work, but will wrestle with a plethora of sometimes conflicting demands on their time. Those who are married will want to spend time with their spouses, who will probably also be Adaptables. They may also be caring for elderly parents or grandparents and/or children. They'll be enrolled in college classes and in other educational activities. Work will be only one of the ways they want to use their time.

Adaptables will be very flexible in their schedules and will expect their employers to be flexible, too. Some may want to work from very early in the morning until mid-day. Others may want to come in during the early afternoon and work later into the evening. Still others, perhaps working from home, will work sporadically during the day, fitting all their business and personal activities into a complicated schedule.

Employers who attempt to strictly enforce working hours, time off, dress codes and similar personnel policies may find themselves unable to attract or hold these highly talented employees. These workers will seek flexibility, rather than trying to adhere to a set of rules that seem arbitrary and senseless.

Alert, Sensitive

These highly sensitive workers will be very alert to problems, opportunities, and subtle changes in their lives or their work environment. This alertness will keep them on the cutting edge of effectiveness.

These workers will be astute at spotting potential problems before they become serious. Quick thinkers, they'll discern solutions and begin implementing them in short order.

They'll be alert for new opportunities, too. Always trying to better their situation, they'll build and maintain a very productive networking system. They'll know what's happening, where, why, when, and how. With their powerful antennae, these folks will be "connected."

Docking to Employer

When we use laptop or notebook computers, we learn about "docking." This descriptive word refers to the process of plugging in to a personal computer or mainframe at a stationary work site. You do what you need to do, recharge, then unplug and move on.

Adaptables will look at their relationship with their employers as a sort of "docking" situation. They'll plug in and get their work done. They'll recharge (learning, growing, gaining credits for their resumes), then they'll unplug and move on to another employers. "Permanence" will not be in their vocabulary.

Family Flexibility

Adaptables will expect their families to be flexible and understanding. They will lead unpredictable lives that will make them seem unreliable and difficult. Actually, they're just anxious to get the most out of life.

Many of these workers may work what we might regard as crazy schedules. They'll change jobs with short notice and may move—even from city to city—rather frequently. This constant movement will work well for the singles and those married to other Adaptables. However, this lifestyle may be hard on their children, which is why many Adaptables will slow down when their children reach school age.

Independence

Adaptables will fiercely defend their independence. They won't want to be controlled by anyone—employer, family, friends, or economic conditions. They will make their life decisions, including career choices, based on what they feel is best for them. While they'll listen carefully to mentors, they'll avoid unwanted outside influences.

Uniqueness, Pride

A strong sense of pride—both for who they are and what they accomplish—will be an observable characteristic of the Adaptables. Each of them will be unique, and proud of that uniqueness. They will deliberately accumulate experiences and expertise that will help distinguish them from anyone else.

Creative Marketer

Many Adaptables will have a keen sense for marketing. They will be proficient at marketing their employers' services, products, and opportunities. They'll demonstrate the same ingenuity in positioning themselves in the talent marketplace.

Using an intuitive sense, they'll apply a high level of creativity to the marketing process. This ability will be seen inside their employment organization, as well as outside arenas where they'll sell their ideas in an almost infectious way.

Intelligent

A strong intellect will enable Adaptables to compete at a high level—in many aspects of their lives. Few workers with "average" intelligence will be seen as part of this elite group. These folks will be smart.

Now, this statement does not mean that all Adaptables will be found in professional positions. Not at all. We'll see many of them in production, maintenance, and service occupations. They'll seek the kind of work they prefer, and may well switch careers even half a dozen times. They'll test styles of work to see what they really like. Income will be important, of course, but they'll be more motivated by finding a job they enjoy.

Aggressive

These will not be shy people. The Adaptables will know what they want, at least for the moment, and they'll go after those objectives with vigor. They will not be pushed around nor told what to do in domineering, confrontational terms.

Adaptables will expect their employers to give them the authority necessary to fulfill their responsibilities. They will have no problem being accountable, but without authority they will leave for more autonomous opportunities. Micromanagers beware! Your practices will not work with these workers.

Sometimes Adaptables will push a bit more than their superiors may like This resistance won't bother the Adaptables; they'll forego tact and diplomacy and fight for what they believe in. If the conflict is too much, they'll simply leave and seek another employment opportunity.

Technological Expertise

Most of these employees will be highly competent technologically. They will have studied computers and other emerging technologies diligently in school, as well as in business-sponsored educational experiences. The knowledge and confidence gained through hands-on application will serve them well.

Communication Skills

With the obvious importance of good communication skills to move ahead in their careers, the Adaptables will become very skillful in writing, speaking, and listening. They will be prolific readers, absorbing all the knowledge they can. Most will share this knowledge comfortably and generously with others, although some may hoard their knowledge for personal gain or provide it only when it works to their advantage.

Adaptables will be sought by some employers because of their communication abilities. More traditional employees may feel threatened by the Adaptables' strong communications effectiveness, especially when that ability moves them into positions of influence very quickly.

High Performer

When given assignments to complete or results to achieve, Adaptables will consistently outperform their counterparts. Tenacious and eager, they'll seek ways to be highly productive. Their objectives will include earning outstanding performance references on every job to help them advance their careers. They'll be out to prove themselves every day.

Well Organized

To accomplish all they want to do, Adaptables will be highly organized—in their personal and in their professional lives. They'll certainly use planning tools like the Franklin Planner® or hand-held electronic planning devices. But the real power of their organization will come from their heightened internal motivation to make the best use of their time.

Unconventional

These unique people will not be conformists. To a large extent, they'll make their own rules and set their own pace. You won't see Adaptables wearing cookie-cutter suits like uniforms. You won't see them spending a lot of their time ingratiating themselves to the boss at a host of social functions. They'll do some of the obligatory socializing, but will grow impatient and bored. These people will be action-oriented.

Renaissance Men and Women

The familiar descriptor relating to an enlightened time in our history will be applicable to the Adaptables. They will be concerned with the development and nurturing of their bodies, minds, and spirits—as a balanced equation that enables them to really "be," not merely exist.

Some Adaptables will have already moved past the creative Renaissance stage into the post-Renaissance period of really applying the knowledge and insight gained and distilled during the late 1990s.

Don't Need Security

Adaptables won't clamor for security in their employment or careers. At least, they won't demand that their security be provided by their employers or other entities. They'll manage their own career security by their performance and movement (growth).

They'll expect to live in a fairly safe community (or they'll work tirelessly to make it safe). Self reliant, they'll take care of their own personal security at home or on the road.

The new breed of workers will remain in a job as long as they feel useful and productive. They'll get the "itch" to move considerably earlier—and more frequently—than ever before. The shift may be within the same organization, to perform much different work. We'll see production workers moving into sales, salespeople moving into management or marketing, administrative workers moving into production.

Adaptables will move to other employers with ease. They'll carry their skills to whatever opportunities seem right for them. They'll look out for Number One, demonstrating temporary loyalty to employers, but permanent loyalty to themselves.

It's difficult to estimate what percentage of the new workforce will be Adaptables. Most of them will be the young up-and-comers, but we'll see a noticeable number of workers in their thirties, forties, and even fifties exhibit at least some of the traits of the Adaptables.

Some workers already in the employment mainstream have wanted to behave like the Adaptables I've described above, but have been hindered by corporate cultures and a perceived lack of opportunities for fast-track movement. Many of these frustrated latent Adaptables have abandoned the corporate world in favor of starting and running their own businesses.

Difficulty in measuring the "frustration factor" limits our capacity to predict what's going to happen as the economy heats up. A probable scenario would see large numbers of Dormant Adaptables coming to the surface. This emergence from the cocoon of conformity will be stimulated by the increasing turnover I see starting in the mid-90s.

Once the Dormant Adaptables take flight like the butterfly, they will not return to the cocoon. They will have their freedom and they'll relish it! These newly-released workers, with their pent-up energy and creativity, could generate the kind of high productivity and accomplishment we saw following the Renaissance.

20

Forecast
Seller's Market
Self
Determination

The labor market ain't what it used to be!

Workers now have control over their careers. More than ever before, workers are in the driver's seat in selecting careers, employers, specific positions, and rate of growth and movement.

In days gone by, there were many workers relative to the availability of jobs. Employers could pick who they wanted to work for them, and, for the most part, decide what positions their workers would hold, what those workers' career paths would be, and how fast they would move along those paths. It was clearly a buyers' market.

Most workers would agree that, over the years, there has been some abuse of the trust they placed in their employers. Employer behavior over the past few years—evaporating loyalty, broken promises, coldhearted decision-making, actions based largely on dollars and cents—dissolved whatever trust was there. This treatment motivated employees to rely more on themselves, rather than depend on others—employers, contractors, agencies, counselors, bosses, or even co-workers.

The labor marketplace is now characterized by more of a "look out for Number One" attitude. Understandably, many workers have become fiercely defensive. . . and offensive to protect their current and future positions.

This reactionary attitude is connecting with an established attitude of independence and self-reliance on the part of the Baby Buster generation. A great many people are listening together to that famous radio station, WII-FM: "What's **In It For Me?**" People will be asking this question, and raising a lot of hard, specific issues, as they assume control and responsibility for their own careers.

Workers will take care of their own benefit programs, negotiating with prospective employers for exactly what they want. Most workers will have substantial benefits programs, offered by mass merchandisers, tailored to their needs and interests. Part of the negotiation between recruiting employers and an interested applicant will be how much of the employee's portable personal benefit package will be funded by prospective employers.

Tomorrow's workers will be looking for a different kind of employment opportunity than they did just a few years ago. They will want more freedom on the job, more growth opportunities (read: training and education), and more judgment of their performance based on skills, competencies, and achievement of results.

As this book is being written, we have already begun to see evidence of workers taking control. In my convention speeches, I talk about applicants interviewing recruiters—a definite turning of the tables in this relationship. When I predict this phenomenon will begin soon, employers in my audiences tell me it's happening already. They tell me about things they've heard from fellow employers, as well as their own personal experiences. A number of these people have told me about applicants asking the very question I predict will be posed: "Why should I work for this company?"

Few employers are prepared to answer that question. Some have even admitted to me privately that they don't really know how to answer the question! If you need to persuade others to join you and you can't convince yourself that your company is a good place to work, you're in trouble!

Shallow answers will not satisfy these aggressive, self-focused applicants. They want depth! They're making their life decisions much more carefully now. These astute applicants are focused on their personal interests and what's best for them. "Self-centered" is considered a positive description in these days of higher personal awareness.

Once employed, the workers of tomorrow won't let up. They will continue to seek opportunities that are good for them, as well as good for the company. The ethics base will be strong enough that most people won't take undue advantage of the employer for their own good, *unless the employer's values and behavior suggest to the worker that taking advantage is the right thing to do.*

These sellers' market employees will *expect* to receive training as part of their employment. And they won't be satisfied with "lick-and-a-promise" training. They'll demand a quality professional development program guided by good facilitators.

This professional growth will extend to all kinds and levels of employees. The lines of demarcation between types and ranks of employees will grow fuzzy, as everyone pitches in to accomplish the work. We'll see a lot more collaboration, with non-management workers assuming as much—or more—leadership than those who are paid to "manage."

Employers will do some different things to hold on to their valued employees. The "sale" made during the pre-employment interview will have to be reinforced, or those employees will be searching for other opportunities before you know it—and there will be a demand for their services.

Some industries will experience serious sellers' market impacts. It will become increasingly difficult for employers to recruit—there simply won't *be* any people outside that door to the hiring office. Once a company's reputation for negative employee relations becomes common knowledge in the community, the company will be hard-pressed to find qualified applicants.

In order to keep sellers' market employees, employers (this means managers, too!) will have to practice pro-active customer relations internally— treat employees as if they were customers. And they will be like customers. . . consumers of the manager's leadership style.

Complications

During the next 5-10 years, we'll observe an interesting circumstance. Sellers' market employees will work side-by-side with employees who don't see themselves the same way. There will be some conflict, including conflict between older-style managers and employees who view themselves somewhat as transient contractors.

The values of one group will be in direct opposition to values held by other groups. There will be several different schools of thought—this values conflict may not be a clear cut distinction. Unless employers are sensitive to this condition—and do something about it, the turbulence caused by this internal conflict could destroy a company.

There will be potentially higher turnover generated by these sellers' market employees. This inability to rely on specific people being around for a long time to fill certain positions will cause employers to systemize even more. The movement to establish standardized methods, expectations, and quality levels will be supported by this lack of continuity.

Some employers may want to recruit the very same employees they let go during the recession or soon after. Many of these folks will be ready (perhaps even eager) to return. Most will respond with a "thanks, but no thanks" when offered an invitation to return. It will be difficult, if not impossible, to rebuild the same strength enjoyed before all the cutbacks. The new strength will be different, and probably a bit more tenuous.

The mixture of the old and the new employees will add to the turbulence. A wide range of emotional feelings will be at work: fear, jealousy, pity, competition, suspicion, pride. Managers and executives will have to be much more sensitive to employee feelings about such concerns as family, pets, free time away from work, etc.

Section 4

Implications
&
Opportunities

21

Position Yourself for the Future

When pilots encounter turbulence in the atmosphere, they often change their flight path to find smoother skies. Why? The most obvious answer is that flying through turbulence is uncomfortable— for pilots as well as passengers.

Constant turbulence is not good for the aircraft, so finding less risky air space is a wise move. Pilots re-position their aircraft by educated trial and error. They tell the passengers about "finding a smoother altitude," but they usually have a pretty good idea just where they're going. They know from past experience, communications with other pilots and air traffic control, and plain old experimentation. They can't see turbulence; they just feel its effect.

Turbulence in the world of work can't be seen, either, but we certainly feel the effects. When we encounter turbulence, it's uncomfortable and perhaps risky, so we reposition ourselves. We do this for ourselves, and for the organizations we're "piloting" through the skies of uncertainty into the future.

Most of us will be doing a lot of repositioning —at our own volition or at the direction of others. In this process, we will be well-served by gaining as much knowledge as we can about our current—and future—environments. Understanding and following trends will provide great insight, especially if you also track other trends that are important to your business and personal life.

To best position ourselves for the future, we must know what our positions are now. We must learn about our vulnerabilities as well as the opportunities available to us. Armed with this knowledge and insight, the rest is up to each of us.

Both corporations and individuals must re-position themselves for future success. In the chapters that follow, well explore the vulnerabilities and opportunities for both organizations and workers. We'll also look at some advice for young people who have yet to enter the world of full-time work.

22

Corporate Positioning

Vulnerability

Every organization, public or private, must consider itself vulnerable in these turbulent times. These vulnerabilities, both external and internal, must be anticipated, so that sound strategies can be proposed and initiated.

External vulnerabilities, from forces outside the organization, are usually beyond the control of its administrators, but affect it nonetheless.

The most obvious threat from outside is competition from other companies. There will be plenty of business available during the next 5-15 years, as we learned in the chapter on the economy. However, many other companies in your field will also pursue the same customers you target. Everyone will strive to maximize their market share.

How will you perform in this era of aggressive competition? How well will you strategize, and how long will you wait before you begin? How will you differentiate yourself from your competition? What resources will it take for you to position yourself where you want to be in your marketplace? If you don't have what you need to be successful in the years ahead, how will you fill your voids?

Another external influence will be technology, both existing and emerging. New technology will develop so rapidly that we must consider it to be an outside factor. We will not be able to protect our proprietary advantage unless we develop our own leading edge technology.

New technologies can be a threat for several reasons. First, of course, is that our competition will gain access to the technology first, create an application plan, and implement it before we do. When that happens—and it often will, our charge will be to add value to the application to make it even more worthwhile for our own usage.

A second threat of rapidly developing technology is that it will be relatively expensive to acquire. . . but perhaps a necessary investment. We will want to have it, but the initial cost will probably be high. Consider the cost of acquisition, of course, and don't ignore the cost of supplanting current technology. Changing systems can be costly.

Advancing technology can also be an inside threat. In most organizations, there will be some resistance to new technology. People become comfortable doing things a certain way and don't like to change. . . especially when it seems like they just changed a short time before. Those resisting will be in conflict with those who are pushing to be on the leading edge of technology application. This internal conflict will cause turbulence inviting mediation by senior leadership.

As we continue to shift applications of technology, retraining may also be a major expense. Wise employers will budget money and time to continually build competence and confidence in how work is done.

Another internal threat is the company's culture, including the style(s) of leadership practiced by management. Organizational culture, simplified, is the expression of the protocols that have been established over a long period of time. The beliefs held by members and leaders of the organization may be inconsistent—there may be disagreement between departments, levels, or functions of the company.

The culture may actually be counterproductive to the achievement of stated objectives. Essentially, the company may be getting in its own way. Few organizations have really looked carefully at their culture to determine how much internal congruence they really have. The messages received by employees about what should be done—how, when, and by whom—may be very confusing.

Culture and management styles can contribute to another serious vulnerability: workforce stability and continuity. Without qualified, experienced, and dedicated workers, employers will have a very difficult time meeting their objectives. Given the trends pointing to an unprecedented churning in the labor marketplace, this exposure is a real and present danger. Most employers are at a much higher risk than they suspect.

Advice

Corporate thinking must shift from "bigger is better" to "smaller is more responsive." Customer expectations and business opportunities must be responded to—and quickly, or they'll be lost to your competition.

I recommend a philosophy that I describe as having a "speedboat" mentality. Speedboat, as compared to battleship. The concern is how nimble and flexible we are, how fast and easily we can respond to opportunities. . . and threats.

Speedboats are highly maneuverable. They can speed up or slow down very quickly. They can make tight turns to change direction. Passengers are closer to the water, to the action.

Battleships, on the other hand, take a while to build up speed or slow down. Their turning radius is very wide, and turns don't happen quickly. The passengers have a better view being much higher, but they're much further away from the action.

The larger and more staid organizations become, the more they become like battleships. They have a lot of strength, but are limited in how well they can engage emerging opportunities or avoid impending threats.

Smaller organizations—or those that think and act in a highly responsive manner—are best likened to speedboats. They pride themselves in flexibility and agility. Response to change is a way of life, whether that change is internal or external.

Larger organizations would be wise to create smaller, more autonomous, business units. Empower and encourage each of those units to create and nurture a speedboat mentality. As they develop the discipline of teamwork with a laser focus on serving customers, these "speedboat" companies will capture their markets.

Not all technology is appropriate for every company. Instead of rushing to adapt whatever is new, carefully assess alternatives to determine what is best for your organization. Stay very clearly focused on your objectives and don't be swayed by fads. At the same time, remain alert to changes that should be made in your company, and implement them as rapidly as possible—with careful planning, of course.

Share your "big picture" with all employees, so they, too, can understand what you are doing . . . and why. Get them involved in the planning, implementation, and evaluation processes—to gain their valuable input and to earn their support. People support what they help to create, so give them lots of opportunities to be a part of the creative process.

Deliberately build and maintain a strong workforce—strong in its capacity to help you achieve—or surpass—your objectives. Raise your standards—for hiring and performance—and insist that they remain high. Once you have hired top talent, do everything reasonable to retain them.

Training and education will be essential elements of organizational success in the future. Learning will be a constant process. To accomplish this success, most employers will have to dramatically upgrade their training programs. Too many companies gutted their training departments during the downsizing in the early 1990s. Now those valuable departments will make an important comeback.

Larger companies will be in a good position to strengthen their training function. However, their efforts will only address a small part of the worker population. As we move into the next century, an estimated 80% of workers will work for companies with fewer than 200 employees. The smaller employers simply won't have resources to establish and maintain comprehensive training programs. Their needs will be great, but the training and development resources will be inadequate..

Employers—and employees—will look for outside training sources to fill the void. Part of the need will be met by independent trainers and consultants who will contract to meet long-and short-term needs. In some cases, they will become long-term partners of employers, serving as contract training departments.

Colleges and universities will be called on to provide more learning opportunities. Some courses will be offered for academic credit, but we'll also see a resurgence in seminars, workshops, and courses sponsored by continuing education departments of these community-based educational institutions. Similar programs will be provided by trade and vocational schools—in their facilities and on-site at the employers' locations.

Trade associations will play a larger role in training and education. On national, regional, and local levels, associations will sponsor learning programs for executive, managerial, supervisory, and technical employees of their member companies. This role will be an important one for associations in need of non-dues revenue to support their budgets. Consolidations have reduced the number of member companies for many trade groups, cutting their dues revenue and limiting their capacity to provide desired services. lobbying will continue to be an important role for associations, but there will be an increased emphasis on providing high-content, results-oriented learning at conventions and through stand-alone programs.

Personal and professional growth will be a major theme for workers during the next 15 years. Employers may be slow in realizing how important this issue is. Some companies will give lip service to training and development, moving slowly into building a strong program to upgrade employee capability. Those employers who move most quickly will gain a substantial advantage—in employee performance, in attractiveness to top quality applicants, and in retaining valuable emloyees they
want to keep.

23

Individual Positioning

Vulnerability

The labor marketplace will become more of a sellers' market, but there will still be strong competition for choice positions. Workers, and I use that term to describe everyone in the workforce—from the entry level employee to the president and chief executive officer, will compete for the opportunity to pursue their desired career path.

We will become less desirable and less effective if we don't continually re-examine and readjust our career development, enhance our knowledge and skills, and take deliberate actions to move ourselves forward. There will be a constant pressure, a tension, for self-improvement.

Some workers will feel the career advancement impetus very strongly, others hardly at all. Along with the fast trackers will be a large number of workers who will continue to "go with the flow" of opportunities that come their way. If you don't decide to assume more active control over your destiny, you probably won't reap the richest rewards the future has to offer. You have to decide whether you want to pay the price.

Relatively rapid movement along the career path will cause some casualties. Some forward-looking employees will be emotionally torn apart by the turbulence in their lives as they have to make very hard choices.

When a wonderful job opportunity attracts you, you'll have to decide if you're going to move to that distant city. What happens to your family? Will they join you, or will they resist yet another move? Where will you place your highest importance—on enhancing your career or on remaining with your family and perhaps achieving less? These gut-wrenching decisions will affect more and more of us. It won't be easy. And the long-term costs of these choices may not be obvious.

We will forever compete against young people entering the workforce with lower salary requirements. . . and more knowledge about the latest technology. Their knowledge from school will be fresh and their attitude will be eager. To compete, we'll have to emphasize our maturity, wisdom, experience. . . and how we've kept up with technology through our own continuing education.

Acquiring our education and training will be a major challenge—consuming time, brain power, and perhaps our own personal funds. Those who don't deliberately grow in their knowledge and skills will simply not be able to keep up.

It's obvious that computer literacy will be essential for future success. Those who are not very comfortable with computers and their use are doomed to limited career growth. This relative ignorance of computers is a serious vulnerability for older workers who already possess wonderful competencies in other areas. Computer use will become like a language—if you can't communicate using the language, all your knowledge and experience have no value.

Advice

Begin now to strategize how you will develop the balance of your career. From the knowledge you currently possess, determine where you want to go as a long-term career objective. Then, plan step-by-step how you will achieve that goal.

Consider what kinds of positions will enable you to gain the knowledge and experience to progressively earn your desired long-term opportunity. Detail, as much as you can, what you want from each position and perhaps how long it might take you to acquire what you want.

Put your plan in writing. Plans that are not written are merely dreams. File the plan with your important papers, perhaps in a specially marked folder that will enable you to find it easily.

Yes, you'll be working with that plan frequently. On a regular basis (quarterly?) you should review your plan to see if you're still on target. Have your goals changed from what you've learned? Do you need to invest as much time with your current employer as you initially believed? More time? Maybe less?

Do quarterly reviews of your plan seem too frequent? That may seem so today, but your attitude may well change as the velocity of your life picks up over the next 5-15 years.

Don't assume that your plan has set in stone. You will change it a number of times as you move forward. Some of your modifications will be in response to opportunities that will become available to you unexpectedly. You may alter your plan because your own ideas of where you want to go will have changed. With all the changes coming in the years ahead, it's wise to be nimble.

Learn. Learn more. Then learn even more. Success in the future will come, at least much more quickly, to those who continually learn. Deliberately acquire knowledge and skills whenever and wherever you can.

Workers will choose employers, in part, based on the learning opportunities that will be available. Negotiate with your employers to pay for, encourage, and support your ongoing professional growth—no matter what kind of position you occupy. Repay your employer by applying your new (and "old") knowledge and skills to strengthen the employer's position and achievement.

Look outside the workplace for growth. Attend continuing education and credit courses offered by colleges and universities. Seek and encourage strong learning opportunities at trade and professional association conventions, seminars, and conferences. An increasing quantity and quality of learning will be available by computer—on CD-ROM and via modem. Take advantage of it.

Learn how to use computers. Enrich your computer skills. Learn how computers are being used—and will be used in the various applications in your career fields. Master those applications so you'll have a good foundation as they move to the next generation.

Since computers will be used increasingly for research and communication, strengthen your skills in these specific applications. Concentrate on improving your writing ability, so you can express yourself better through electronic mail and similar interactive communication media.

Foster an attitude of being highly responsive, flexible, and willing. Treat every relationship as though the other people involved are your customers and you're in business for yourself. Share your feelings about your career development with your family and friends and solicit their support. Stay focused on what you want to achieve.

Develop and apply an attitude of giving 100% to your employer. Your employers will be hard-pressed to accomplish all that lies before them to be done. Employees who genuinely put forth strong effort will be sincerely appreciated and rewarded in many ways. Perform well and you will be considered a valuable team member.

Prepare yourself to work in the emerging environments of home-based employment, satellite work stations, and the virtual world. At some time in your career, you may be asked to function in these new ways—or you may find an opportunity that will put you in one of those environments. Practice working alone to get a job done, but also strengthen your ability to work interdependently with others. . . in close physical proximity, across the country, or around the world.

Become involved in community service work. Experience as a volunteer will give you a wonderful laboratory to practice your interpersonal skills and enhance your leadership abilities. You'll build relationships outside of work that may well help you advance your career. And, you'll gain the feeling of satisfaction that you made a difference for yourself and others.

Work with a professional coach and/or ask friends to give you honest and critical feedback. Don't allow yourself to be complacent with who you are. The increasing velocity of life in the foreseeable future suggests that stagnation will put you far behind faster than you might imagine.

24

Advice for Young People

Often after I give speeches at conventions and corporate meetings, I am queried by individuals from my audiences who want to talk with me one-on-one. Many of them are parents seeking my counsel, as a futurist, on how to advise their children who are still in school.

My advice for these young people is to acquire a broad base of knowledge. Learn about history, but appreciate why things happened even more than what happened. Discover how fields of knowledge developed. Gain an understanding about how various disciplines relate with and influence each other.

Develop an inquiring mind that empowers you to ask the kinds of questions that provoke deep answers. Look beyond the surface; continually ask "why." Learn how to be creative. Creativity is, at least partially, a developed skill.

The most rewarding opportunities in the future will involve things we don't even dream about now. As rapidly as technology is developing today, our young people will mature in an even faster-moving work environment. Students who focus their education too narrowly will find themselves confined to their specialties. Bright minds should not have limitations.

Become conversant in a wide range of subjects and fields of discipline. Be equally comfortable with the arts, humanities, and sciences. Be lighthearted, yet serious about your studies. Strive to master each subject, earning higher academic achievement and a more solid foundation for future learning and application of knowledge.

Develop your communication skills. Through courses and extra-curricular activities, learn how to speak well—conversationally, as well as formally.

Learn to write well. You should be able to easily compose letters, memos, articles, and reports. The finest knowledge and understanding has no value if it can't be communicated to someone who will use it.

Read books and magazines in a wide range of fields. The best advice I ever received, 'way back when I was in high school, was to read magazines from many fields on a regular basis. While I may not be familiar with all those fields in depth, I have a general knowledge of what's happening and what's important to the people around me.

Strengthen your listening skills. Your ability to listen well will be one of your greatest assets. Whether you're in management, sales, research, production, service, or any other occupation, you need to be able to listen to learn who people are, what they want, and how you can best interact with them.

Enhance your social skills. Acquire the capacity to mix comfortably with all kinds of people —at all levels and from any background. As diverse as our country—our world—is, your enhanced social skills will serve you well. Learn to communicate with different kinds of people without prejudice and you will position yourself well for future success.

Invest some of your time in community service. Aside from the societal value of volunteerism, you will gain personally from the experience. Learn and practice leadership skills, sensitivity, patience, and enthusiasm. You   see, volunteer leadership teaches you how to get people to do things when you don't have "control" over them. Those persuasive abilities will serve you in other areas of your life. Experience the exhilarating feeling of making a significant difference in the lives of others.

The most successful people in the future will be those who can relate well with others, who can be flexible, and who have a wide range of interests and understandings. Those who concentrate on one specialty area without gaining a broader background will find their opportunities very limited.

Closing Statement

Well, here it is. All the way at the end of the book. . . as an afterthought. So much has been said about "paradigms" over the past few years, the term has become another buzzword of our times. Some of my clients and people I've met at conventions have really tired of hearing the word.

So, I wrote this entire book without using the word. . . until now. We can't completely ignore it. Thanks to Joel Barker, the once-obscure word now has significant meaning for a lot of people, especially corporate leaders, futurists, students, and management consultants who will read this book.

Yes, we are talking about shifting paradigms. All of us will experience dramatic changes in our lives as a result of the turbulence in the work environment. We'll look at things much differently—almost on a daily basis!

Some employers will become paradigm pioneers, eagerly and aggressively searching for new and better ways to do things. It's already happening. And those efforts are causing turbulence within those organizations. Some can handle the turbulence just fine—they expect it, practically embrace it.

Other employers, and people within all organizations, are experiencing, and will experience, the frightening discomfort of turbulence that can result from paradigm shifting. In many cases, this uneasiness will flow from a lack of communication or buy-in to the transformation process.

Genuine paradigm shifting has to be done throughout the organization. It can't be accomplished by just one small group with an expectation that everyone else will follow along.

Unfortunately, the established pattern in most corporations, government agencies, and not-for-profits is not inclusive. This paradigm must change in order that all the rest of the paradigm shifts might be effective.

Wise employers will educate their people about trends, paradigm shifts, and turbulence so they can know what to expect. Remove the suspicion and uncertainty through open communication and wondrous things can happen.

If I were consulting with you on how to proceed, I'd encourage you to talk openly with all your employees about the concepts in this book. Depending on your size, you may need to meet with a number of groups of employees—for *discussion*, not a lecture from the boss. Invite questions. . . and solicit solutions. Your front-line people may have more insight and solutions than the folks in the executive suites—at least about some of the issues that are relevant to them.

Begin looking more strategically at how your organization and your field/industry will be affected by what the future will bring. Form future study groups comprised of different kinds of employees from varying fields and hierarchical levels in your organization. Engage a professional futurist firm for research and stimulation services. If you need recommendations of firms to consider, call me at (216) 836-5656 and I'll suggest a few.

If you'd like to order multiple copies of this book to distribute to your people, your customers, and/or your suppliers, give us a call. We'll be glad to arrange a quantity discount purchase to help you move your organization deliberately into the future.

The years ahead will excite and challenge you in ways you never expected. . . or prepared for. Managing people and organizations will be unconventional, because everything around us will be shifting. Enjoy the turbulence. It will be a new experience and you'll be able to make a real difference with your leadership.

Hang on! It's going to be a wild ride!

Have fun!

About
the Author

Roger E. Herman is best described as a "business futurist." As a Professional Member of the World Future Society, he watches a wide range of trends. His particular areas of concern are issues that affect the workplace and workforce. Armed with this information and insight, Roger educates and advises corporate leaders throughout the United States and overseas. His support enables his clients to better position themselves for successful futures.

A substantial part of Roger's work is done on his feet as he shares his perspectives with corporate and association audiences in his role as a professional speaker. Roger has delivered speeches and seminars full-time since 1980. The National Speakers Association recognizes him as a "Certified Speaking Professional." As this book is published, only 246 people in the world have been granted this designation.

Roger's consulting clients appreciate the fact that the Institute of Management Consultants has validated his work by accrediting him as a "Certified Management Consultant." As of this writing, 1,580 people have been awarded that distinction in the United States. There are approximately 20,000 Certified Management Consultants in 19 countries.

In addition to his speaking and consulting, Roger is also an internationally-published author. This book is his fifth, complementing his publication of over 500 magazine and journal articles.

Roger's fourth book, *Keeping Good People,* was published by McGraw-Hill in English (hard and soft cover), Spanish, German, and Portuguese. It was featured by the Business Week Book Club and the Newbridge Executive Book Club. This well-received book on employee retention is also available as a 6-tape audiocassette album. *Keeping Good People* is now distributed in a trade paperback edition by Oakhill Press.

The Process of Excelling is Roger's other business book. Described as a "practical how-to guide for managers and supervisors," the book presents the twelve elements of successful organizational leadership. Copies of this book are available through Oakhill Press.

Roger holds a Bachelor of Arts degree in Sociology from Hiram College, Hiram, Ohio. His masters in Public Administration was granted by The Ohio State University in Columbus. He grew up in the Maryland suburbs of Washington, D. C. Roger's military service was fulfilled as a Counterintelligence Special Agent for the US Army.

Roger is president of Herman Associates, Inc., a management consulting and training firm based in Akron, Ohio. Formed in 1980, the firm serves organizational clients throughout the United States. Most of the firm's professionals are Certified Management Consultants.

You can contact Roger Herman through his office by calling (216) 836-5656. The fax number is (216) 836-3311. His mailing address is Post Office Box 5351, Fairlawn, Ohio 44333 and his e-mail address is: 75473,2217@compuserve.com.

INDEX